Intercultural Communication

The Essential Guide to Intercultural Communication

Jennifer Willis-Rivera

University of Wisconsin—River Falls

BEDFORD/ST. MARTIN'S

Boston ♦ New York

Manufactured in the United States of America.

4 3 2 1 0 9
f e d c b

For information, write: Bedford/St. Martin's, 75 Arlington Street, Boston, MA 02116   (617-399-4000)

ISBN-10: 0-312-55190-8
ISBN-13: 978-0-312-55190-2

PREFACE

The Essential Guide to Intercultural Communication is a versatile supplement that examines how one's cultural background informs identity development, both verbal and nonverbal communication, as well as the complexities of intercultural communication within organizations; the text also discusses how different cultures are portrayed in mediums of popular culture.

WHY AN *ESSENTIAL GUIDE TO INTERCULTURAL COMMUNICATION?*

Gone are the days when most people socialized, received an education, got married, and had a family in the same town or region in which they were born. Today, because we are more physically and virtually mobile, we interact with people of different cultures from all around the world. In addition, the demographics of our own communities at home are becoming more culturally diverse due to less restrictive and less discriminatory immigration laws, the overturning of anti-miscegenation laws, and the increased freedom to be an out LGBTQ individual, among other social and cultural changes in the United States. A working knowledge of intercultural communication is crucial for successful and competent communication in today's increasingly culturally sensitive world.

Certainly in the communication discipline, intercultural communication is a growing area of study and research, and many departments now require that courses like human and interpersonal communication cover culture, either as an integral component woven throughout the course or as an individual unit. While books for these general courses often do include coverage of culture, sometimes more information is needed. Although cost and time constraints make it unrealistic to require both a general-survey text plus another specifically on intercultural communication, I felt there was a need for a concise guide that provided students with a strong framework for understanding the basics of intercultural communication, written in a way that engaged students and satisfied instructors' teaching needs. However, I would not consider myself entirely honest if I did not admit that I also wanted to write this guide for personal reasons: I am a Caucasian woman married to a Latino man, and we have two biracial children. My professional interests are influenced and strengthened by the fact that my family and I negotiate and deal with intercultural issues—like multiracial identity and prejudice—everyday.

In my many years of teaching, I have discovered that students often connect to challenging ideas and theories through the use of relatable examples. Many of the examples I use in this book are drawn from common observations that students may be aware of but may not have considered—like the "rules" of arguing or why women are perceived as more emotional than men. I also look to sources of popular culture that students are familiar with, such as the film *Bend it Like Beckham* or the viral video of "Dancing Matt" on YouTube, to supplement and illustrate what I teach. I also share insights into my own experiences with intercultural communication—like stories about the development of my twin daughters' multiracial and multiethnic identity—because I have found that students respond well to personal anecdotes that help them see the tangible effects of intercultural communication in their lives. By discussing intercultural communication in situations that people deal with on a daily basis and by using examples rooted in real life, these theories and concepts come alive for students.

STRUCTURE AND COVERAGE

The Essential Guide to Intercultural Communication is divided into seven chapters and includes coverage of the following topics.

- Clear definitions of culture, communication, and intercultural communication (Chapter 1)

- A discussion of how various aspects of verbal communication, like meaning and grammar, as well as nonverbal communication, like proxemics and chronemics, are rooted in one's culture (Chapter 2)

- A thorough examination of how culture influences identity formation, from the multiple aspects that shape our identity, like race and gender, to the different stages of minority, majority, and multiracial/multiethnic identity development (Chapter 3)

- An explanation of the idea of crossing borders and cultural shock—concepts unique and pertinent to the study of intercultural communication (Chapter 4)

- A look at how intercultural communication works in the context of relationships and within organizations (Chapter 5)

- An exploration of popular culture—movies, television, books, toys—and how it both overtly and covertly influences the way people perceive their own, and others', cultures (Chapter 6)

- Five things that students should remember and practice in order to engage successfully and critically with intercultural communication (Chapter 7)

Culture permeates every facet of our lives. Therefore, in addition to learning the core principles and theories of intercultural communication, it is also key for students to be able to translate what they learn in the classroom into their own lives. *The Essential Guide to Intercultural Communication* also gives students practical advice on how to be more critically aware of their intercultural communication so they can continue to learn about, and engage with, culture and become more effective communicators.

This booklet is available either as a stand-alone text or packaged with *Real Communication: An Introduction, Reflect and Relate: An Introduction to Interpersonal Communication,* and a number of other Bedford/St. Martin's communication titles, including the booklets *The Essential Guide to Rhetoric, The Essential Guide to Presentation Software, The Essential Guide to Interpersonal Communication,* and *The Essential Guide to Group Communication.* For more information on these or other Bedford/St. Martin's communication texts, please visit www.bedfordstmartins.com.

There are many people without whom this book could not have been written. I must thank my family—my husband Daniel, and my children Arcelia and Micaela—for your love, encouragement, and endless supply of examples. Thank you also to my friends, colleagues, and my great students—especially my student assistant, Eric Douglas, who read through every word to make sure I didn't sound too "old." I am grateful to everyone at Bedford/St. Martin's who supported this book: Joan Feinberg, Denise Wydra, Erika Gutierrez, Erica Appel, Karen Schultz Moore, Adrienne Petsick, as well as the incredibly helpful project-editorial team: Shuli Traub and Kellan Cummings. Finally, special thanks goes to my editor Ada Fung, for prodding me when I needed it, and helping to create this book.

Jennifer Willis-Rivera

CONTENTS

Defining Intercultural **1** *Communication*

What do you think about when you hear the term "intercultural communication"? Like many people, your mind might wander to a French businessperson interacting with a colleague in the Tokyo office, or a professor from England lecturing to her American students. But culture encompasses more than the country we're from or the language we speak. It also involves race, gender, religion, geographic regions, and a host of other factors. Even two individuals of the same race who grew up in the same town attending the same house of worship will find that they have certain cultural differences that affect their communication with one another. The fact is, cultural differences are a very real and relevant part of our daily lives.

The purpose of this book is to give you a taste of this incredibly pervasive nature of intercultural communication by examining our verbal and nonverbal communication, our personal identities, our borders and boundaries, our interpersonal relationships, our organizations, and popular culture. My hope is that by reading this text, you will see everything you do — how you speak to your grandmother, how you chat with friends when sitting at a diner, or how you dress for an important speech — through the lens of culture. To begin this process, I use this introductory chapter to define the basic building blocks of intercultural communication, and these definitions serve as a foundation for the rest of the text. I also incorporate many examples from my own experience which, I hope, will elucidate my points and give the reader a sense of where I am coming from and my own take on intercultural communication. That said, let's move on to these all important definitions.

WHAT IS CULTURE?

Before we can get into the details of intercultural communication, we need to have a clear understanding of what "culture" means. As we've noted, religion, race, educational background, and so on are specific parts of culture. But, more broadly, **culture** is a "socially constructed and historically transmitted system of symbols and meanings pertaining to communication" (Philipsen, 1992, p. 8). That is a packed definition, so let's break it down further, and examine the assumptions underlying that definition.

CULTURE IS SYMBOLIC AND CHANGEABLE.

First, let's examine the idea that culture is a "system of symbols and meanings" (Philipsen, 1992). A **symbol**, in the most basic sense, is something that represents, or is associated with, something else. For example, words are specific arrangements of letters that we as a society have determined stand for a particular object or idea. For example, P-E-N is known to English speakers as an ink-based writing instrument. There is nothing inherent in those letters that says we must use them to describe said writing instrument, so we could decide to use the letters D-U-C-K to represent the ink-based writing instrument instead. You might argue that we already have a water bird named D-U-C-K, but, in English, there are words that share the same construction but have different symbolic meanings (O-R-A-N-G-E stands for both a fruit and a color).

Culture is symbolic. Some of these symbols of a culture are very visible and obvious, such as a country's flag. Others are less obvious because they seem so "natural" to people. An example of this would be raising your hand in class when you want to ask a question. Why do we raise our hand? We could just as well raise both hands, stand up, or raise our foot! Those options may all seem silly, but really, they could have the same effect as raising your hand. We raise our hand because, in the United States, that is the symbol we, as a society, have decided on as a means for getting attention in the classroom. In fact, we could make the same argument for most of the ways people interact in their everyday lives.

Symbols are often embedded with a multitude of meanings that shape, and are shaped by, a culture. For example, let's look at the flag of the United States. Certainly, most people living in the United States know that the stars on the flag symbolize the fifty states, and the stripes represent the thirteen colonies. However, the flag holds even deeper cultural symbolism in the United States. Many believe it stands for freedom and bravery; for some it symbolizes sacrifice and battle. Think about the rules we are taught regarding how to treat the flag. Is it really that important to respect the flag, as an object? Of course not. As an object, the flag consists of colored bits and pieces of material and thread. What matters is the *symbolic* significance of the flag. The flag is a symbolic representation of a nation, and by treating a flag with respect, we are symbolically treating the nation it represents with respect.

While certain objects may hold a symbolic cultural meaning, culture is not an object that someone can simply pick up or point to and say "this is culture." Culture, in some ways, defies a static and fixed definition. We can give the word "culture" a definition, but we can't say exactly what the culture of a particular group of people *is,* because it changes so frequently. We can't describe Dutch culture today by using descriptions of Dutch culture from one hundred years ago. Nor can we necessarily say that one interpretation or aspect of Dutch culture represents the whole culture. So in this way, we must respect that culture is changeable and malleable. Culture is symbolic, and symbols are open to interpretation—some people may look at a symbol one way and some may look at it in a slightly different way.

Someone once described to me the metaphor of culture as a single frame in a movie. Culture can be defined as a particular way in a particular time, but by the time you stop to examine that moment in time, it has already changed. We can see this progression very clearly in language. Over a few generations in the United States, "cool" has come to mean that something is good or hip, and not necessarily that something is cold. Also, if someone says you are "sick," that means you are awesome, and not ill. The meanings, that is, the cultural understandings of these words, have changed over time. We can also see this change in meaning in other signifiers of culture. Bronzed or tanned skin in the United States has changed from a symbol of the working class, from a time when people had to work outside in the sun all day, to a symbol of wealth, either from affording exotic vacations or spending money for tanning salons. In this example, the cultural symbolic meaning has moved significantly— from one end of the spectrum to the other—over the past one hundred years.

CULTURE IS A SOCIAL CONSTRUCTION.

As I suggested earlier, societies decide the cultural meaning of certain symbols. Therefore, we can also conclude that culture is a **social construction**, which essentially means it is created by a society. However, it isn't created in the same way that a building is created. A building is carefully planned and measured before ever being built. Cultures are created, for the most part, unconsciously. Cultures don't assign representatives to sit around a table and "decide" what that culture is going to be like. Culture is constructed without our actively thinking about it; it is constructed by our interactions with each other (Jackson, 2004). So, because we repeat particular actions or speech patterns, like dressing little girls in pink and asking people "How are you?" these patterns become embedded as part of our culture. If culture is socially constructed, then by that definition, culture isn't biological—it isn't determined by your genetic structure. That means that physical characteristics do not determine cultural background. This is an important distinction to establish, because gender and race are part of culture—but not because of genetics. Certain genetic cues (color of skin, shape of eyes, sex organs) have been socially constructed to have particular meanings.

When we describe women as a cultural group, we might say "women cry more than men do." However, consider this point on a biological level. Do women cry more than men because they have more active lacrimal glands? Is it because they produce tears differently than men do? Hardly. Women appear to cry more often than men because tears have a different social meaning for women than for men. Boys in the United States are taught at an early age that crying is something they should not do. When boys are hurt (emotionally or physically) they are often told in various ways to "get over it." Girls, however, are not given that same script: when they are young, they are often held and asked to talk about why they are crying. They are encouraged, in this manner, to express their feelings. Given this difference, men and women grow up with differing emotional reactions to stimuli. Men might refrain from crying because they were taught that it's not "masculine" to do so, whereas women might not have those same qualms. Therefore, it could be that women cry more, not because of biology, but because the different meanings assigned to tears in the different genders mean it is more socially acceptable for them to cry.

I'm not attempting to use this example to deny the biological differences between men and women. Biologically, men do have a different makeup than women: they generally have more muscle mass, less body fat, and higher testosterone and lower estrogen levels, along with a different reproductive structure. However, those biological differences do not account for all, or even most, of the ways cultures differentiate beteween men and women. The same is true for racial differences. Race may appear to be a biological characteristic, but scientists have not been able to isolate single genes (or groups of genes) that can differentiate one race from another. Society has taken particular physical markers such as hair color, eye color, and eye shape and assigned a meaning to them called "race." We discuss in more depth in Chapter 2 the fact that race and gender, while having innate, inborn aspects, are still socially constructed cultural groups.

CULTURE IS LEARNED AND PERFORMED.

Though this isn't stated specifically in our definition of culture, the idea that culture is learned follows from the idea that culture is socially constructed. Since culture is not in our genes, we must somehow learn about culture. For example, in the United States, we are taught to drive on the right side of the road and to ask questions in class if we don't understand something. These behaviors are not "natural" or "normal," they are aspects of culture that need to be taught. In the United States, these rituals are "correct." However, in other cultures, these rules may not be true, and in fact opposite behaviors may apply.

In addition to being learned, culture is also *performed* every day. This is different from the kind of acting one would do with a script on stage. For example, when American children get dressed up in costumes and go trick-or-treating during Halloween, they are performing the ritual of that particular holiday. Our everyday actions, like greeting someone by shaking their hand, are also cultural performances. We may not think of an action like shaking hands as a cultural performance because it seems so "natural." However, culture is only alive and active through the performance of it. If no one is "doing" the action anymore, that is, if people suddenly stopped shaking hands as a sign of greeting, then it would cease to be a part of our culture. This brings us to the idea that in order for certain aspects of culture to remain present they must be reinforced and passed down from generation to generation.

CULTURE IS REINFORCED AND GENERATIONAL.

In addition to being learned and performed, aspects of culture are also reinforced so there can be no doubt that they are both purposeful and meaningful. If certain rituals or activities are not reinforced, then they just become one-time occurrences or chance happenings that have no prolonged meaning. The meanings we attach to colors are a great example of how culture is reinforced. For example, in the United States, pink is a color that has culturally been attached to girls, while blue has been attached to boys. I have twin daughters, and I will never forget the time a complete stranger chastised me for not dressing my then-infants in pink so she could tell they were girls! This stranger took it upon herself to reinforce this particular value that she felt I was violating, which shows just how pervasive this symbol is. Another example of this is holiday customs—just try telling someone you're vegetarian and won't eat turkey on Thanksgiving. You might very well hear, in response, "But you have to eat turkey, it's Thanksgiving!" In fact, cultural values are reinforced to the point where they become common sayings—from "big boys don't cry," which dictates how one should behave as a male in the United States, to the understanding that little girls are made of "sugar and spice and everything nice," which reinforces how one should behave as a female in the United States. People growing up in any culture can reflect back and come up with many examples of similar assumptions that are strongly reinforced in their culture.

If culture is reinforced, then it is safe to say that culture is also **generational**—it is passed down in society from generation to generation. Therefore, if culture is generational, then it is not the same as a **fad**, an idea or item that is enthusiastically followed or coveted by a group of people, but only for a short amount of time. For example, Beanie Babies are a fad. They are something that, aside from existing in a handful of collections, will be all but gone in one hundred years. However, the overarching idea of collecting, that is, gathering up at least one of everything in a set, is cultural. The value in collecting different types of objects is an idea that is passed down from generation to generation in United States society—even if the value of the specific object being collected is not.

CULTURE IS INTERNALIZED.

I mentioned previously how some cultural symbols or cultural performances seem so "natural." This is because culture is often **internalized**, which means that many of our cultural performances and symbols have become so instinctive to us that we don't see them and we don't think about them—they simply exist within us. We don't think of our everyday actions as cultural, we think of them as "normal," because we are immersed in and surrounded by our own culture. The saying "Does a fish know it's wet?" illustrates a similar idea—a fish lives in water, and therefore may not recognize that it is wet. However, the term "normal," when used to describe cultural practices, can be problematic. The fact that people in Britain drive on the left side of the road is no more "normal" than the fact that people in the United States drive on the right side of the road. A bride wearing white on her wedding day in France is no more "normal" than a bride in China wearing red. However, because people grow up immersed in the "water" of their culture, everything that culture does seems to just be the "right" way to do it and everyone else seems either odd or wrong. This can lead to a great deal of misunderstanding among cultures, when people from one culture judge the behaviors of others by their own cultural standards.

CULTURE IS INSTITUTIONAL.

Not only are cultural actions and symbols internalized, they are also **institutional**. In other words, our cultural norms—how we work, play, and live—are built into our institutions: into our schools, into our organizations, into our government, and into the whole of our society. I mentioned earlier in the chapter that culture is reinforced, and institutions are a big part of this. A simple way to think about this is to look again at the cultural norm in the United States of driving on the right-hand side of the road. This cultural norm is built into, and reinforced by, many systems of our government. If you are caught violating this norm, you will likely receive a ticket and a stern talking-to from a police officer. This is how the legal institutions of our country reinforce the norm of driving on the right-hand side of the road.

Another example of how culture is institutional can be seen in the educational system. For example, when you want to use the restroom during class time, you typically ask for a bathroom pass or for permission to leave the room from the teacher. While there are no legal ramifications if you violate this particular norm, it is something that is taught and reinforced in schools throughout the United States. If you don't ask for permission, you may get punished or reprimanded by your teacher. This idea is so built into our school system that it has become "normal" to ask permission before going to the restroom at school, but it is important to understand that this may not be "normal" for other cultures. In the film *Mean Girls* (2004), Cady, the protagonist, has just begun school at an American high school after years of homeschooling in Africa. She is seen getting reprimanded for just getting up to go to the bathroom on her first day, because doing so is "normal" to her. As we can see from these examples, culture is not just internalized by individuals, but by institutions as well. A cultural group decides what behaviors and actions are considered "the norm," and that cultural group's institutions often take part in reinforcing those behaviors and actions.

WHAT IS COMMUNICATION?

Now that we've taken a look at how culture is defined and the assumptions that go along with that, let's examine how culture pertains to communication. First, we will look at what we mean by communication, and then we will answer the question: Why is communication crucial to the definition of culture, and vice versa?

Communication is the symbolic exchange of meaningful verbal and nonverbal messages. We will examine this in greater depth in later chapters, but basically we communicate with people both verbally (through language systems) and nonverbally (through nonlanguage systems). We can communicate with people by talking to them, but we also communicate with people through body movements, the clothes we wear, our facial expressions, and so on. It is important that when we talk about communication, we understand that both of these aspects of communication are at work at all times.

Now, let's go back to the use of the word "meaningful" in the definition of communication. This is an important piece of the definition because communication is only communication because it is perceived as meaningful. **Perception**, that is, how we interpret and understand a message, is the most important part of communication, whether the message sent is intentional or unintentional. For example, if your friend waves to you as she passes you by, and you don't see her so you don't wave back, she may perceive that you are mad at her. Your intention (you didn't see her) isn't the crucial part of the communication; it is her perception (you are angry at her) that will frame your next encounter. Communication must be meaningful. If no one ascribes any meaning to an interaction, no communication has taken place. If you sneeze, I might make no meaning of your action, and therefore, no communication has taken place. But, if you sneeze and I start to worry "Oh no, he's sick. I can't get sick. I need to stay away from him," I have assigned meaning to your actions, which puts them in the realm of communication. I am ascribing the meaning of "you are sick" to your sneeze. Whether you have a contagious virus or are simply suffering from allergies is of no importance. The meaning I ascribe to it — my perception of the communicative event — is what changes an action into communication.

WHAT IS INTERCULTURAL COMMUNICATION?

We have defined culture, and we've defined communication, but we have yet to put those two together. What is intercultural communication? **Intercultural communication** is communication with or about people of different cultural groups. I specifically include "about" because when we talk about a particular cultural group in a particular way, we are sending a message about what that group is like. For an example of this, let's look at perceptions of, and communication about, male culture. If a child watches a cartoon on television showing a male figure as an inept parent (for example, not knowing how to change a diaper, not watching after the children carefully), the underlying assumption communicated is that men are not capable of taking care of children. This assumption is repeated over and over again in numerous media sources (for example, the cartoon *Rugrats,* the film *Daddy Day Care,* and so on). While one might argue that the males in these situations are "only acting" or the situation is only "make believe," it is people's perception and what they might take away from the message presented (men are bad at taking care of kids) that is important. When this image of men as inept parents is repeated frequently in the media, this perception of men becomes internalized and institutionalized. It becomes okay to laugh at it because we all "get" the joke—men are not as good as women at taking care of children. When we communicate about a particular cultural group, we are creating a perception of that group—so whether they are physically present or whether you are actively communicating with that group or not, it is still considered intercultural communication.

WHY SHOULD WE STUDY INTERCULTURAL COMMUNICATION?

Now that I've explained what I mean by intercultural communication, the next question is: Why study it? What is it that makes intercultural communication an essential and growing branch of the communication discipline? Intercultural communication has been a vital and fascinating subject for me for many years, and I'm always eager to pass on that excitement. There are three main reasons why the study of intercultural communication is important: the global village, self-awareness, and awareness of others.

INTERCULTURAL COMMUNICATION AND THE GLOBAL VILLAGE

The term "global village" was popularized by Herbert McLuhan in 1962. He used this term to describe how mass media were collapsing time and space barriers in our world so that interactions with people from around the world would become more and more frequent. Certainly that is true in society today; the Internet, e-mail, and instant messaging make communicating with, and learning about, people around the world much quicker and easier. People in many parts of the world also have a greater ability to travel than ever before. We meet people from other cultures far more frequently than our grandparents or great-grandparents ever did—perhaps more than they ever dreamed we could.

The global village has become part of the workplace (Zakaria, 2000; Sullivan, 2002). People from many different cultural groups may work in the same company or office, each with some differing customs, ideas, and assumptions that seem just as "normal" to them as yours do to you. When we gain an understanding of intercultural communication, we are better able to see these cultural differences for what they are—differences. Not weird or abnormal beliefs or behaviors, but simply different ones.

In understanding intercultural communication in the workplace we are able to also adapt our own cultural practices when necessary. The global village as workplace also means that our jobs themselves may traverse cultural boundaries. Often, companies have branches or interests in other regions and/or other countries, each with their own cultural groups and cultural practices. Not only can an understanding of intercultural communication help you to recognize that these "strange" practices are merely different cultural norms, but knowing that can help you to better adapt to these new cultural demands. As a student of intercultural communication you will become more keenly aware of both the verbal and nonverbal aspects of communication, and be better able to pick up on subtle nuances.

The global village is also a factor in relationships. According to the United States Census, interracial marriages are on the rise, the percentages of interracial marriages having more than doubled from the 1990 census to the 2000 census (Edmonston & Lee, 2005). Interfaith marriages are now fairly common as well. Over time, it will become very likely that most people will know someone who is involved in an intercultural relationship, or be involved in one themselves. Having an understanding of intercultural communication can help you to be aware of issues that intercultural relationships might face.

INTERCULTURAL COMMUNICATION AND SELF-AWARENESS

Another reason to study intercultural communication is to become more self-aware. I mentioned earlier in this chapter the saying "does a fish in water know it's wet?" In studying intercultural communication, you are the fish studying the water around you, and therefore becoming more aware of it. Often, people of a majority culture see themselves as not having a culture at all, because everything they do, say, or think is just "normal." Culture is seen as an exotic aspect of "other" people. After reading this chapter, you know this isn't true. We are surrounded by our culture, and culture is pervasive in nearly all of our actions. Ruth Frankenberg (1993) did a study where she interviewed white United States women about their race, and found that, for the most part, these women did not feel they had any cultural or racial place, because they were so normalized into their culture that they couldn't see it or feel it. Since Frankenberg's study, other scholars have found similar attitudes (Nakayama & Martin, 1998; McIntosh, 2004).

Studying intercultural communication helps us to see our own actions through the eyes of a stranger. We are seeing our performances in the same way we might view others' performances. When we are able to view our own actions as cultural, we cease to use the word "normal" in our descriptions of those actions. Many of the stereotypes and judgments that exist for minority cultural groups highlight the "abnormalness" of the group from the dominant culture. A description of such "abnormal" behavior is given by Miner (1956) as he talks about a little-known tribe in North America, the Nacirema:

> The daily body ritual performed by everyone includes a mouth rite. Despite the fact that these people are so punctilious about the care of the mouth, this rite involves a practice which strikes the uninitiated stranger as revolting. It was reported to me that the ritual consists of inserting a small bundle of hog hairs into the mouth, along with certain magical powders, and them moving the bundle in a highly formalized series of gestures. (p. 506)

If you didn't realize it before, this culture, Nacirema, is "American" spelled backwards, and Miner is describing the process of brushing one's teeth. This act is so normal and natural to this group of people, they probably do not think of it as a cultural practice. But of course it is! Not all cultural groups approach dental hygiene in the same way, and some practices may seem odd, if not disgusting, to other cultural groups. Through studying intercultural communication, we become self-aware enough to understand our own cultural practices as just that, and we are better able to understand and accept the cultural practices of others without judging them.

AWARENESS OF OTHERS AND INTERCULTURAL COMMUNICATION

When some people think of studying intercultural communication, they may think it is simply studying how to be politically correct. This is not the case. **Political correctness** is generally referred to as speaking or acting in an inoffensive manner, especially with regard to race, religion, sexual orientation, and so on. While it is important to be considerate of others in intercultural communication, political correctness can be problematic because in some ways it prevents open and honest intercultural communication. People may be afraid that in trying to understand and see the viewpoints of others, they might come across as offensive and branded as "politically incorrect" — something that may not have a positive connotation in their own culture. Many people argue that political correctness causes us to have to think about the words we use so carefully, it can be prohibitive to learning and understanding other cultures (Wilson, 1995; Fairclough, 2003). As students of intercultural communication, you will find that intercultural communication is not about simply being politically correct. It is about coming to a much deeper understanding of the meanings and contexts of cultural practices and cultural traditions.

Political correctness implies that there is a strict "correct" and "incorrect" way to be, so I am proposing an amendment to that term. Instead of "political correctness," why not "political kindness"? This term places the emphasis on being considerate, rather than simply being "correct." Political kindness means more than being politically correct for the sake of being inoffensive; it means critically examining the underlying assumptions we have of our own and others' terms, ideas, practices, and traditions. When we do so, we are able to understand that these cultural elements do not exist in a vacuum, but are, in fact, inextricably linked to a person's understanding of who she or he is. In recognizing that, we are much more likely to act toward others with understanding, and yes, kindness.

Anne Frank (1947/1993) ended her diary with the words "In spite of everything, I still believe that people are really good at heart" (p. 263). Learning about intercultural communication and understanding the implications and assumptions that underlie all of our communication with and about the "other" can remind us to act with our good hearts and to be cognizant that others have good hearts when we communicate.

REFERENCES

Edmonston, B., & Lee, S. M. (2005, June). New marriages, new families: U.S. racial and Hispanic intermarriage. *Population Bulletin: A Publication of the Population Reference Bureau, 60*(2). Retrieved from http://www.prb.org

Fairclough, N. (2003). 'Political correctness': The politics of culture and language. *Discourse and Society, 14*(1), 17–28.

Frank, A., & Roosevelt, E. (1947/1993). *The diary of a young girl* (B. M. Mooyaart-Doubleday, Trans.). New York: Bantam.

Frankenberg, R. (1993). *White women, race matters: The social construction of whiteness.* Minneapolis: University of Minnesota Press.

Jackson, R. L. (2004). Cultural contracts theory: Toward a critical-rhetorical identity negotiation paradigm. In P. Sullivan and S. Goldzwig (Eds.), *New approaches to rhetoric* (pp. 89–108). Thousand Oaks, CA: Sage.

Lee, S. M., & Edmonston, B. (2005). New marriages, new families: U.S. racial and Hispanic Intermarriage. *Population Bulletin, 20*(2), 1–36.

McIntosh, P. (2004). White privilege: Unpacking the invisible knapsack. In P. S. Rothenberg (Ed.), *Race, class, and gender in the United States* (6th ed., pp. 188–192). New York: Worth Publishers.

McLuhan, M. (1962). *The Gutenberg galaxy: The making of typographic man.* Toronto, Ontario, Canada: University of Toronto Press.

Miner, H. (1956). Body ritual among the Nacirema. *American Anthropologist, 58*(3), 503–507.

Nakayama, T., & Martin, J. (1998). *Whiteness: The communication of social identity.* Thousand Oaks, CA: Sage.

Philipsen, G. (1992). *Speaking culturally: Explorations in social communication.* New York: State University of New York Press.

Sullivan, J. J. (2002). *The future of corporate globalization.* Westport, CT: Quorum Books.

Wilson, J. K. (1995). *The myth of political correctness.* Durham, NC: Duke University Press.

Zakaria, N. (2000). The effects of cross-cultural training on the acculturation process of the global workforce. *International Journal of Manpower, 21,* 492–510.

2 *Verbal and Nonverbal in Intercultural Communication*

As I mentioned in the last chapter, communication is both verbal and non-verbal. Most people differentiate between these two terms by whether or not something can be heard. While that covers most aspects of the definition, it isn't entirely accurate. In communication studies, we differentiate between these two concepts by language use. **Nonverbal communication** takes place without the use of **language**, that is, words or symbols that are governed by a grammatical system. **Verbal communication** uses language. For example, sign language, which most people think of as nonverbal communication, is actually verbal communication because it uses language. On the other hand, the sound of your voice (the rate, tone, pitch) is nonverbal communication. In this chapter we will look at how culture influences and is influenced by both verbal and nonverbal communication.

VERBAL COMMUNICATION AND CULTURE

Culture and the cultural groups we belong to influence our verbal communication, from the words and language we use, to the way we phrase and use those words. In this section, we look at how usage of words and grammatical structure can differ between cultures. We also consider the format of conversations and arguments, as well as the roles they play in different cultures.

WORDS AND MEANING

One of the first things people think of when it comes to interacting with other cultures is language. Often, when we travel to different countries, language barriers are one of the first difficulties we are faced with. What may not come to mind is how language can vary within our own country, and how it affects intercultural communication when we ignore the more subtle differences in language and simply assume we speak the same language. In some parts of Wisconsin, the term "bubbler" is used for a drinking fountain. I remember the first time I heard this term, I had no idea what the person was talking about! Although we both spoke English, "bubbler" was a regional term I was not familiar with. Or, you might drink "soda," "pop," or "coke" (all of which are generic terms for soft drinks) depending on which geographic region of the United States you are from. People will often get into debates over which term is the "correct" term; Facebook is filled with groups proclaiming each of these terms as the "correct" one. Of course, given what you learned in Chapter 1, you know there is no "right" or "wrong" term — they are simply different because they are specific to a particular cultural group.

Not only might different cultures have different terms for the same object or notion, a specific word can have different meanings or connotations for different cultures. We, as a society or cultural group, have the ability to change words to mean different things. Simply because we have decided that a particular arrangement of letters means something doesn't mean we can't change it; in fact, we do that all the time! We change the meaning, or create multiple meanings, of words ("chilling" isn't always done in a refrigerator) and we create new ones ("chillaxing" is a combination of chilling and relaxing). Because people can change a word's meaning, some cultural groups may use a word in a different sense from its dictionary definition. An example of this would be the word "queer." The literal definition of queer is something that is strange, or unusual. Unfortunately, it has been used in the past as a derogatory term against the LGBT (lesbian, gay, bisexual, transgendered) community, but in recent years, some members of the LGBT community have chosen to actively reclaim and reappropriate the term "queer" and use it in an empowering fashion to represent a sexual orientation or gender identity/expression that is not strictly heteronormative.

GRAMMAR

The grammatical structure of language is also culturally bound. You may already be aware that languages differ in their grammar structure. For example, in the English language, adjectives generally come before nouns, whereas in Spanish, it's the exact opposite. So, instead of "blue house," you would say "casa azul" in Spanish, which translates literally as "house blue." While this example may seem like just a matter of difference in grammar between the two languages, there are some grammatical distinctions between languages that are a reflection of larger cultural differences.

In the English language, there is really only one form of the word "you." Albeit, there are some regional permutations of the word, like "y'all," but that is still seen as a synonym for the more common "you" in the English language, rather than a word that has a different meaning or connotation entirely. However, having a singular word for "you" is not the case for all languages. For instance, in the Spanish language, there are two words for "you" — one used for someone you know well, the other used for someone you don't know as well, or for formal occasions. In the United States, the single term for "you" reflects the cultural value of egalitarianism (Kramsch, 1998). It is culturally acceptable in the United States for any person to talk to any other person with little change in their speech. People might use titles such as "Mr." or "Mrs." or

"Dr.," but generally the words you use are the same, regardless of the degree of familiarity or the hierarchy.

The United States is a country with a **low power distance** (Hofstede, 1983), which means that people expect to be viewed largely as equals in society, and the fact that we don't have distinctions between a formal "you" and an informal "you" reflects that. On the other hand, in a **high power distance** country, people expect hierarchy and status to matter in society. For some high power distance countries, that importance is reflected in their grammar. For example, in Japan, people are expected to use a different version of "you" in conversation based on the seniority, age, and social position of the other speaker (Ishihara & Cohen, n.d.). Understand that this isn't simply a case of having an extra word for "you." The fact that there *are* different forms of "you" suggests that there is an entirely different tone and communication style used when addressing someone who is your equal, as compared to someone who is "above" you, in cultures with a high power distance.

These differences in grammar and the larger implications those differences have can certainly impact intercultural communication. Imagine a conversation between Sam, an older man from a high power distance culture, and Mateo, a younger man, from a low power distance culture. Sam may become offended if Mateo does not use what he perceives as the proper tone or communication style in addressing him. Sam may think that Mateo does not respect him, while Mateo may be completely unaware that Sam is feeling this way. It is important for students of intercultural communication to be cognizant that a language's grammar structure can have larger cultural implications and indications, so as to avoid misunderstandings like the one in the example above.

CONVERSATION

The subjects we converse about and the way we converse are also culturally distinct. Think about the topics you bring up in order to initiate a conversation with someone. In the United States, people often begin a conversation talking about the weather, because it is considered safe in almost any situation. Also, people in the United States are taught not to talk about religion, politics, or income because these topics are considered to be quite personal, and off-limits unless you know the person you're conversing with very well. However, it is important to be aware that these conversational norms do not apply to all cultures. For example, in Australia, talking about politics is as common as talking about the weather is in the United States, and in China, it is considered polite to talk about salary or marital status (Martin & Chaney, 2006). As you might imagine, American travelers in these countries might feel offended when people they don't know well start to ask them questions about politics. The perceived offense in this case doesn't stem from the actual words spoken, but from the choice of topic.

Another cultural aspect to consider is the structure of a conversation. Let's look specifically at turn taking, or the way we decide who gets to speak when in a conversation, as an example. In the United States, conversation is marked by frequent turn taking (Mesthrie, 1999). Even when a conversation that is more focused on one person than the other (for example, your best friend is telling you about a party she went to last night), there are often frequent interjections and/or questions from the other person (Gardner, 2001). However, in some other countries, like Finland, longer, uninterrupted, conversational turns are the norm (Tryggvason, 2006). You can imagine how a continuous back-and-forth conversation pattern can be confusing for people from other cultures where long conversational turns are the norm!

As you can see, the "rules" for appropriate topics of conversation and conversation structure can vary from country to country. "Correct" conversation etiquette in the United States may not apply to another culture, and it is important to recognize, and be aware, that these differences are cultural.

ARGUMENT

Argument is another aspect of verbal communication that intercultural scholars study. Not only is the role that argument plays in a society cultural, but how we structure an argument is cultural as well. People in the United States tend to avoid confrontation if possible because people who argue, especially those who raise their voices and argue vehemently, are often perceived as more aggressive (Davidson, 2001). However, this concept might be baffling to people from cultures where argument is simply a part or process of everyday conversation. In fact, in some countries, such as France and Germany, argument is often used as a friendly way to communicate with others (Althen, 1992). This is not just a cultural difference between countries — people in the southern parts of the United States are much more likely to avoid argument, even changing topics to avoid an argument, whereas people in the northern United States are much more likely to engage in verbal dueling. Men also are much more likely to engage in verbal argument than are women (Martin & Chaney, 2006).

Argument structure can also differ between cultures. In many Western cultures, what is considered a "good" argument follows a very linear structure, beginning with a claim, followed by supporting evidence. A logical argument should go from point A to point B to point C, with a clear and distinctive line of thought from one point to another. However, this structure for a "good" argument is not necessarily one that prevails across all cultures. Many cultures, like those of Taiwan and China, use an **indirect style of communication** (Ting-Toomy & Kurogi, 1998), where speakers purposefully do not directly state their main point out of respect to the person they are speaking with. To many people from Western cultures, this might seem incomprehensible. In the United States, we often say "get to the point" when people are taking too long to move from one part of their argument (or story) to another. However, in other cultures, to ask someone to come to the point of the argument in such an overt manner would be rude. Essentially, you would be saying that the person you were communicating with was too stupid to figure out the main point out on his or her own. Our choice of words, what we speak about, and how we structure our verbal interactions convey more than the words' message; they are imbued with cultural values and understandings that are so embedded we don't think about them. To many people, the way we make a point in an argument or the topics we discuss are simply part of "normal," everyday conversation. However, as I mention in Chapter 1, the term "normal" can be dangerous; if we aren't aware that these small but significant aspects of language are in fact cultural, rather than "normal" or "abnormal," it can result in a great deal of intercultural misunderstanding.

NONVERBAL COMMUNICATION AND CULTURE

When we communicate, we use more than our words or our language. Body language, tone of voice, and other nonverbal aspects can communicate just as much, if not more, about a person's cultural background, or a cultural group. In this section we take a look at accent, eye contact, gestures, emotion, proxemics, chronemics, and haptics and discuss why it is important to examine these nonverbal cues with regard to intercultural communication.

ACCENT

Our **accent** is how we pronounce different vowel and consonant sounds in particular combinations. You can see an example of different accents in the different emphasis and pronunciation of the vowel sounds in the word "rodeo." When pronounced in the Midland accent (considered "standard speech" in American English), the letter "e" is pronounced with a long "ee" sound, and the emphasis is on the first "o." However, when it is pronounced in a Spanish accent, the letter "e" sounds like a long "a" sound, and that is the vowel that is emphasized. Why are accents important to study in intercultural communication? Looking at how people perceive different accents and the meaning we attach to accents helps us understand our communication with and about other cultures, as well as be aware of prejudices we might have that can be attributed back to differences in accent and the meanings we assign to accents.

We don't just encounter these different accents and pronunciations across different languages; there are many different accents within a single language as well. In the United States, there are many regional accents, so someone who lives in Alabama might have a completely different accent from someone who lives in New York. People have attached meanings and stereotypes to the various regional accents. People with southern accents tend to be viewed as less intelligent, while people with northeastern accents are perceived to be more abrupt. People with a mainstream United States accent, which is sometimes seen as having "no accent," are often seen as upper-middle or upper class, as literate, and as aspiring to upward mobility (Lippi-Green, 1997). These meanings and stereotypes have become so entrenched in our collective consciousness that we may no longer realize why a specific accent conjures up a specific connotation. By extension, our communication with people we perceive to have an accent different from ours can be colored with these pervasive meanings and stereotypes. A study by Davila (1993) found that Mexican Americans who were perceived to have an accent were paid less than those who were perceived not to have an accent—in other words, they spoke with a mainstream United States accent. The Mexican Americans who were perceived to have an accent were also paid less than those who had distinguishable German and Italian accents.

Certainly, people often rely on regional accents in the United States to help figure out which part of the United States someone is from. However, always assuming that someone's accent is a sign of where they are from can be problematic, because it is possible for someone to have an accent that is identified with a particular region or country, but they may not consider that region or country home. This is particularly troubling for those who have accents that are perceived as "non-American." Even if someone has been an American citizen for a long time, and considers the United States home, they can still be perceived as a "foreigner," and their belonging and citizenship can be constantly called into question if they have any trace of a "non-American" accent. While accents might be a part of a person's identity, it is important to remember that there are many facets to identity, and that someone's accent should not be seen as the whole representation of their identity.

The values and meanings we might place on different accents can also affect our ability to listen. For example, people who have Australian accents are often seen as exotic by people in the United States, while people who have Spanish accents are often seen as uneducated. People will often try harder to listen to what they consider to be an exotic or interesting accent than they will a more negatively coded accent. When people hear an accent that is not held in high esteem, they will often "shut down" any attempt to listen, or will at least not try as hard as they would with an "attractive" accent. As students of intercultural communication, you should be cognizant of the fact that the connotations and values attached to someone's accent inevitably color our communication with that person. If we don't stop and recognize that those meanings are arbitrary and cultural, our future communication of and about people who have similar accents can also be affected.

EYE CONTACT AND GESTURES

Eye contact, like all other forms of communication, conveys meaning that is culturally specific. In the United States, people are taught that making direct eye contact is generally a good thing because it communicates respect and that you are paying attention to the person speaking. In a job interview, your interviewer may feel suspicious if you aren't looking directly at him or her, and might feel that you either don't care about getting the job, or are hiding something. Most parents in the United States demand their children look them directly in the eye when they are being disciplined. Lack of eye contact, for many in the United States, communicates disrespect, lack of attention, or dishonesty. On the contrary, in many Latino cultures, direct eye contact is considered a challenge to authority, not a sign of respect. Also, in some other countries, like Japan, prolonged direct eye contact with a superior (such as in a job interview) would be seen as very rude (Nishiyama, 2000). Some cultures consider direct eye contact between men and women passing on the street as a sexual invitation, yet direct eye contact between strangers when walking on the street is nothing more than an acknowledgment of presence in the United States.

Gestures are another, often overlooked, nonverbal cue that can cause significant misunderstandings. Due to the fact that many of the gestures we use on a daily basis are like second nature to us, we often don't think about what that gesture might mean when taken out of its cultural context. What is a commonly used gesture in one culture may not mean anything at all, or be thought of as rude, in another culture. For example, in the United States, we might think nothing of pointing at someone or something to call attention to it. However, in most Asian countries, it is considered rude to point at someone or something. Gestures that have positive connotations in one culture may have negative connotations in others. The "OK" sign (the forefinger creates a circle with the thumb with the other three fingers splayed out) is a positive gesture in the United States — it signals that everything is going fine. However, in Japan this sign means "zero" or "money." In Spain, it means someone is sleeping with your spouse. We might assume that the universal gesture for "yes" is to move your head up and down, and the universal gesture for "no" is to move your head from side to side. However, that's not the case! In Bulgaria it's the exact opposite, though the "no" is typically a quick nod up, rather than up and down multiple times as "yes" is in many other cultures. As you can imagine, the differences in the meaning of certain gestures or of eye contact across cultures might cause some awkward misunderstandings! While it is not possible, or even expected that everyone know every culture's understanding of a certain gesture or of eye contact, it is important to simply recognize that differences exist, and to be sensitive of them.

PROXEMICS

Proxemics is the study of the invisible bubble of space around us, or what is commonly known as our "personal space." Anthropologist Edward Hall (1966) identified four **proxemic zones**, or zones of personal space, that are typically observed by people in the United States: **intimate space** (from zero to eighteen inches), **personal space** (from eighteen inches to four feet), **social**

space (from four feet to twelve feet), and **public space** (over twelve feet). Therefore, it is considered culturally acceptable for people you consider to be quite close with you, like your significant other, best friends, or close family, to be within eighteen inches of yourself, but not someone you just met at a party. Certainly, most of you probably would feel uncomfortable, worried, or even defensive, if someone you were just introduced to insisted upon cozying up to you; according to Hall's proxemic zones, it would be more acceptable for that person to be in your personal space, anywhere between eighteen inches and four feet. However, it is important to recognize that these are generalizations for the United States that Hall makes based on his research and observations. In other countries, the demarcation of these distances can be very different. For example, in many Latin American countries, a comfortable distance between acquaintances is much less than the comfortable distance for people in the United States (Salzmann, 2007). Also, in many northern European cultures, the proxemic distances are much larger than in the United States, so if you were to meet someone from a northern European culture, you might find that standing even two feet away from them isn't quite enough distance to make them feel comfortable.

A person's preferred personal space is not visible, and therefore hard to read. However, it is important to remember that proxemics does communicate meaning, like degree of intimacy or comfort, and is often reflected through other body motions. For example, when we feel like our personal space is being invaded, the emotions we might experience inside, like defensiveness or worry, might be reflected in a tense voice and stiff body posture. Being sensitive to these cues will help you be cognizant of your own and others' proxemics, which, in turn, will allow you to recognize when you are violating someone else's personal space. Simply because you are standing in relation to someone else in a way that makes you comfortable, does not mean the other person is comfortable.

CHRONEMICS

Chronemics, the study of how we use time, is a fascinating area of nonverbal communication. Communication scholars have found that there are two general cultural views of time: monochronic and polychronic. (Hall & Hall, 1990). A **monochronic** view means that time is seen as linear and constantly moving forward and the past is generally thought of as having little impact on everyday goings-on. The United States, as well as some northern European cultures, where promptness and adhering to a schedule or predetermined plans are valued, are considered monochronic cultures. People in the United States tend to live by the clock; it tells them when to get up, when to go to work or class, when to eat, and when to go to sleep. In fact, the United States has many idioms that revolve around time, like "time is money," "a day late and a dollar short," and "early to bed and early to rise makes a man healthy, wealthy, and wise." U.S. society and institutions in the United States tend to reinforce what is seen as appropriate or "correct" chronemics. For example, teachers and schools will often penalize students if they are late to class, and companies probably won't offer you the job if you are late to the interview. Time is seen as a valuable commodity, as shown in the AT&T commercial in which a mother pulls her son's "minutes" (represented physically by little orange discs) out of the trash and admonishes him for throwing them away, and essentially wasting his cell phone minutes.

On the other hand, a **polychronic** view of time means that time is seen as more flexible and cyclical and that past events have an impact on the present and the future. Southern European, Middle Eastern, Latin American, and Native American cultures are polychronic cultures, and because they tend to view time as a more fluid entity, they are less likely to compartmentalize or organize their time as most monochronic cultures do. People from polychronic cultures have a high commitment to relationships, and value these relationships over promptness. For example, to end an interaction with someone just because the clock says it is time to leave would be seen as rude.

You can certainly see how these very different viewpoints on time can cause significant problems in intercultural communication. If, for example, a student is frequently late for class, it could be because that student is from a polychronic culture, and doesn't feel that this is a problem. However, an instructor from a monochronic culture may perceive the student as lazy or not caring about the class. Understanding how time operates in cultural situations may help avoid making hasty conclusions about a person's intentions when it comes to time.

HAPTICS

Haptics is the study of touch, a necessary aspect of our everyday lives. While we all use touch in a variety of ways every day, cultures can generally be categorized into three groups — high, middle, and low touch — depending on the degree to which most individuals within the culture use touch. **High touch cultures** tend to use touch frequently in interpersonal interactions, whereas **low touch cultures** avoid touch in most interpersonal interactions. **Middle touch cultures** use touch less frequently than high touch cultures, but more frequently than low touch cultures. The United States and Japan are examples of low touch cultures, France and India are examples of middle touch cultures, and most Latin American and Middle Eastern countries are high touch cultures. Therefore, in a high touch culture, people generally respond positively to touch in most situations, whereas in low touch cultures, people generally respond negatively to touch in most situations. So if you were visiting a low touch culture, and put your hand on someone's upper arm or clapped them on the shoulder to show solidarity, you would likely get a negative reaction rather than the positive one you may have been expecting. You can see how not understanding this could have serious effects in an international negotiation situation in business or politics!

Let's look at forms of greeting to illustrate why studying haptics is important in intercultural communication. One of the most common forms of tactile greeting is the handshake, and in the United States, a firm, but not painful, handshake is considered a sign of confidence. A gentle handshake might communicate that you are weak. However, in Australia, a weak handshake is the very definition of a proper handshake! Which hand you use to shake hands is also culturally specific. While there are no hard-and-fast rules in most cultures, in many Middle Eastern cultures, you should only shake hands with the right hand, as the left hand is saved for unpleasant tasks, like going to the bathroom. Kissing is also a typical form of greeting, particularly in high touch cultures. While it might be fairly common in high touch cultures to greet friends with a kiss on the cheek, in middle touch and low touch cultures, kissing is reserved for romantic/sexual touch, or touch between close family members, like between a parent and a child (Martin & Chaney, 2006). It is not the intended meaning, but rather the perceived meaning, that has the most bearing on communication. So if you give someone you are introduced to a quick peck on the cheek, thinking you are simply being welcoming and friendly, that kiss could be interpreted by the other person as a flirtatious action. It is important, as students of intercultural communication, that we learn to look at our nonverbal behaviors through the eyes of a stranger, and recognize the multiplicity of meanings a single behavior can have. This is not to say that everyone should learn all the possible meanings for each and every form of touch so as to avoid misunderstandings — that would be virtually impossible! Simply recognizing and being aware that your actions might mean something other than what you intend can help you see that there is no "correct" or "incorrect" way of behaving, and prevent you from jumping to conclusions about the "appropriateness" of someone else's behavior.

REFERENCES

Althen, G. (1992). The Americans have to say everything. *Communication Quarterly, 40,* 413–421.

Davidson, M. N. (2001). Know thine adversary: The impact of race on styles of dealing with conflict. *Sex Roles: A Journal of Research, 45*(5/6), 259–276.

Davila, A., Bohara, A. K., & Saenz, R. (1993). Accent penalties and the earnings of Mexican Americans. *Social Science Quarterly, 74,* 902–915.

Gardner, R. (2001). *When listeners talk: Response tokens and listener stance.* Amsterdam, Philadelphia: John Benjamins.

Hall, E. T. (1966). *The hidden dimension.* Garden City, NY: Doubleday.

Hall, E. T., & Hall, M. R. (1990). *Understanding cultural differences: Germans, French and Americans.* New York: Intercultural Press.

Hofstede, G. (1983). National cultures in four dimensions: A research-based theory of cultural differences among nations. *International Studies of Management and Organizations, 8,* 46–74.

Ishihara, N., & Cohen, A. D. (n.d.). *Strategies for learning speech acts in Japanese.* Retrieved March 3, 2009 from University of Minnesota Center for Advanced Research on Language Acquisition, http://www.carla.umn.edu/speechacts/japanese/IntroToSpeechActs/ForTeachers.htm

Kramsch, C. J., & Widdowson, H. G. (1998). *Language and culture.* New York: Oxford University Press.

Lippi-Green, R. (1997). *English with an accent: Language, ideology, and discrimination in the United States.* New York: Routledge.

Martin, J. S., & Chaney, L. H. (2006). *Global business etiquette: A guide to international communication and customs.* Westport, CT: Praeger.

Mesthrie, R. (1999). *Introducing sociolinguistics.* Edinburgh: Edinburgh University Press.

Nishiyama, K. (2000). *Doing business with Japan: Successful strategies for intercultural communication.* Honolulu: University of Hawaii Press.

Salzmann, Z. (2007). *Language, culture, and society: An introduction to linguistic anthropology* (4th ed.). Boulder, CO: Westview Press.

Ting-Toomy, S., & Kurogi, A. (1998). Facework competence in intercultural conflict: An updated face-negotiation theory. *International Journal of Intercultural Relations, 22*(2), 187–225.

Tryggvason, M. (2006). Communicative behavior in family conversation: Comparison in the amount of talk in Finnish, SwedishFinnish and Swedish families. *Journal of Pragmatics, 38*(11), 1795–1810.

Identities in Intercultural Communication *3*

Before I begin talking to my students about identities in intercultural communication, I often start by referencing the song "Who Are You?" by The Who. I have students write a list of how they might answer that question. Many write their names or the roles they have in their lives (sister, brother, student, and so on). Others write personality descriptors (outgoing, shy, optimistic), and some write cultural descriptors (white, Catholic, African American, gay). This exercise helps my students to think in the broadest way possible about their identities. What about you? How would you answer that question?

DEFINING IDENTITY

Identity is how we view ourselves, as well as how others view us, and it is ever changing and complex. Numerous factors, such as race, sexuality, gender, and religion, affect how we answer the question "Who are you?"—and how others attempt to answer the question for us. Let's take a look at a few factors that influence how we define ourselves, including our beliefs about what others think about us and our unique combinations of identity factors from race to sexuality to ethnicity.

THE LOOKING GLASS THEORY

Charles Cooley (1922) argued in his **looking glass theory** that how we see ourselves is shaped by how we think others see us. In other words, we look to others to see ourselves just as we look in a mirror to see our reflections. But please note the importance of the second part of that definition—"how we *think* others see us"—meaning our perception of others' opinions. We can never truly know what someone else thinks unless they share their honest thoughts. However, we make assumptions about people's thoughts all the time, often automatically. At different points in your life you might say "Wow, I bet she thinks I'm really dumb," or "I wonder if he's interested in me? He really seems to like me." Looking glass theory holds that once you make these statements and assumptions they become part of your identity: "I am dumb" or "I am likeable."

But who are the "others" in our definition? George Herbert Mead, a contemporary of Cooley's, introduced the idea of two kinds of "others"—the generalized other and the specific other (1934). The generalized other is the world at large or society in general. When you're getting ready in the morning and your hair just doesn't fall right, you might look at yourself and think "Ugh, what will people say when they see me?" "People" here is the generalized other. If you were to say "What would my mother say about my hair?" you're referring to the specific other—a particular individual. Depending on the situation, generalized others or specific others may have more or less power in shaping your identity. For example, if you view your uncle as an intelligent, successful person, your thoughts about how he perceives your intelligence might matter more to you than what you imagine your classmates think about how smart you are.

OUR MULTIPLE IDENTITIES

There are many factors that shape our cultural identities and make us who we are. We might identify with a race, ethnicity, gender, class, religion, age, sexual preference, and so on—and all of these differences impact us on a daily basis. As with many other factors that affect our communication, we're not always conscious of how our race or religion or age operate in each and every interaction we have. We don't necessarily head into class on a given morning thinking "Today I will answer my professors' questions with the knowledge that I am a nineteen-year-old white, Italian-American, Catholic student with two siblings and divorced parents." However, as students of intercultural communication, we know that it's important to examine aspects of our identities that we take for granted or see as normal and commonplace. It would be impossible to discuss every single aspect of identity in this book, but let's take a look at three aspects: race, ethnicity, and gender.

Race

When I discuss **racial identity**, that is, the race with which an individual identifies and/or the race with which others identify that person in class, I will bring up a current event—perhaps an issue from local or national politics. After we discuss the issues for a minute or two, I turn to a Caucasian student in my class and I ask, "What do white people think about this issue?" This exercise may seem jarring, but it often sparks an incredibly fruitful discussion. My classes are 95 percent Caucasian; I myself am Caucasian. As members of a majority culture in the United States we often don't consider ourselves as having a "race"; we are not expected to answer for white people's opinions, thoughts, or beliefs. This exercise often encourages some of my African American and Asian American students to share that they are frequently asked to explain the thoughts of members of their race, as though all Asians or all African Americans share the same opinions. This example points back to the larger question I brought up at the beginning of this chapter—asking the question "Who are you?" If you are a member of a minority race, you're likely to answer that question with a sense of your racial identity at the forefront because it is salient and relevant. It's something that people are constantly pointing out. But if you're the member of a majority race, you might not even consider it as part of your identity. It's just "the norm." This issue becomes even more challenging when an individual has a somewhat ambiguous race. Instead of "Who are you?" the question becomes "What are you?" Theorist Kenneth Burke (1966) argued that people are categorizing animals. If we can't immediately tell what someone's race is, and hence categorize them (white, Latino, Asian, and so on), we often will question that person until our curiosities are satisfied. Hence, both questions (Who are you? and What are you?) can become central to shaping racial identity.

One very important thing to understand about racial identity is that it is socially constructed, just as the meanings of verbal and nonverbal communication are. Some may argue that because we can "see" differences between people (for example, hair texture, eye shape, skin color, and so on), then certainly these differences between races must be biological. But while variations for curly hair or straight hair and brown eyes or blue eyes are certainly in our DNA, scientists are unable to classify our genes as "black," "white," or "Asian," or any other race. An excellent example of this social construction is to look at the racial categories on birth certificates. My husband was born in the United States to a Nicaraguan mother and a Puerto Rican father, yet he is listed as "White" on his birth certificate, not "Latino" or "Hispanic." He was born in the late 1960s in San Francisco, and "Latino" and "Hispanic" weren't choices on birth certificates—his mother had a choice between "Black" and "White." When our own children were born in the late 1990s, we were able to select their race among a list of six or seven choices. However, we were told that we could not choose more than one race, and "Multicultural," "Other," and "Biracial" were not among the choices. So, we had to choose between "Hispanic" and "White" for our children, even though they are both. As you can see from what is and isn't listed on birth certificates through the years, race is a category that changes with time, rather than a set, biological truth.

Ethnicity

Racial identity and ethnic identity are often used interchangeably. However, there are key differences between the two. As we discussed above, racial identity is a socially constructed and enforced system. We define race as something visible—something that, for the most part, can be identified by looking at a person's hair, eyes, skin color, and so on. **Ethnic identity**, on the other hand, involves someone's national and/or cultural heritage. This is different from race, as people who consider themselves to be of the same race may claim vastly different ethnicities. People of German, Norwegian, Finnish, and Swedish descent may all be categorized as white, but may identify very different ethnically. Ethnic identity is also generally a more personal choice, especially for Caucasians (Bhatia, 2007). For instance, my own ethnic heritage is Italian, French, English, and Welsh. Most of my family members are English, but I was raised to identify with my Italian heritage in terms of the foods and customs that were part of my early family life. For this reason, I choose to describe myself and affiliate most with my Italian ethnic identity.

Latinos seem to face some unique challenges in terms of defining ethnicity. As I mentioned earlier, the terms "Latino" and "Hispanic" are often used to describe someone's race when their family ancestry is Mexican, Puerto Rican, Guatemalan, and so on. Yet, Latinos can also be categorized as members of other races. There are Hispanics who are considered racially white (Cameron Diaz, Martin Sheen), Latinos who are considered racially black (Roberto Clemente, Sammy Davis Jr.), and Latinos who are considered racially Asian. Many Latinos are a mix of these differing races. Therefore, the terms "Latino" and "Hispanic" are more descriptive as ethnic identities than racial identities. Yet how people use these terms is far from clear-cut. Richard is a racially black man with strong ties to his family in El Salvador. When he is asked his race, he defines himself as "Hispanic." Elisa is a racially white woman whose father was born in Mexico. When asked her race, she identifies as "White," though she would consider "Mexican" to be part of her ethnicity, along with Irish, French, and Italian. As you can see, the issue of race vs. ethnicity can largely come down to personal choice. Yet it is an issue that someone whose race is white and ethnicity is German or whose race is Asian and ethnicity is Chinese may not have to consider on such a complex, detailed level.

Gender

Gender is another variable that shapes our cultural identities. At the outset, I want to explain that **gender**—the socially constructed idea of what is masculine and feminine—is not the same thing as **sex**—our chromosonal biologically assigned makeup and reproductive organs. Our biological sex is determined for us; our gender is shaped by what the world around us tells us about being masculine or feminine. You might well be aware of some of the larger ways in which gender identity affects your daily life. For example, women are encouraged to be feminine by giving affection and sharing feelings, while men are encouraged to be masculine by "being tough" and showing no emotion. Such hard-and-fast rules about appropriate gendered behavior certainly evolve over time, yet they can also creep into seemingly innocent places. For example, I remember playing the game of Life with my two daughters when they were young. If you aren't familiar with the game, you choose a small peg (a pink peg or a blue peg) and you place it in a little car and "drive" your way across the board to various milestones in life: marriage, a new job, first house, first child, and so on.

When my daughters started the game, I was intrigued to find that they both immediately chose the pink ("girl") peg and placed it in the passenger seat of the car. I asked them why they didn't place the peg in the driver's seat, and they responded with a shocking statement: "Once girls get married, they don't drive any more." Anticipating the inevitable "get married" turn in the game, my girls were simply saving time and moving their peg to the "appropriate" place for a married woman — next to her husband, who is controlling the vehicle. How did such beliefs come about? In my own life, my husband does most of the driving (simply because I do not enjoy it). This simple act became a gendered behavior in the eyes of our children. Other families may assign gender differences in determining who takes care of the family finances or who prepares the family's meals. Two individuals may get married and find they have differing expectations as to who should mow the lawn or take care of the children, depending on their assumptions about gender roles and view of his or her gendered identity.

Additional Variables That Shape Identity

There are many other variables that affect how we see ourselves and how others see us. Sexuality, class, religion, and age all play a part in defining identity. Consider how your socioeconomic background and your choice of dress might influence how others approach you. In the well-known film *Pretty Woman,* Julia Roberts's character is refused service at a high-end boutique on Rodeo Drive because of how she is dressed. The salespeople perceived from her clothing that she probably didn't have the money to shop at their store. In turn, their judgment made her feel self-conscious of her lower-class status. Similarly, the ways in which we incorporate religion into our lives (or how we don't) also shape identity. How do people in your community view others who wear a Christian cross or Jewish yarmulke or who do or do not attend religious services?

How individuals view their sexuality — and how they attempt to discern others' sexuality — is also a part of cultural identity. Some people argue that they can tell when someone is gay by the way that individual talks or walks or dresses. Usually this involves a man or a woman defying gendered stereotypes (for example, a man who has a higher-pitched voice or wears great shoes). Ezra Tuaolo, a former NFL player who is openly gay, contradicts gay stereotypes. Tuaolo's physical build and profession would certainly fit the definition of "masculine male," yet his sexuality is not what many would assume at first glance. How others perceive your sexuality might influence your identity to the point that you make changes to your appearance in order to "correct" misunderstandings. If you are straight and others perceive you as gay, you might choose different dress, different jobs, different activities, perhaps even different mannerisms. If you are gay and people continually assume you are straight, you might make similar changes depending on the perception you want others to have of you.

Age influences identity throughout the lifespan — particularly when it comes to verbal and nonverbal communication. Age affects the words you speak (few people in their forties or older understand the meaning of "phat"), the gestures you use (two fingers held up mean very different things to a five-year-old, a twenty-year-old, and a sixty-five-year-old), and how you understand the cultural world around you (do your grandparents hold views similar to yours on gender?).

IDENTITY DEVELOPMENT

Now that we understand a bit more about the factors that define and constitute our cultural identities, we can begin to examine how identities are created by us and for us. In addition, we can examine minority identity development, majority identity development, as well as multiracial and multiethnic identity development.

AVOWAL VS. ASCRIBED IDENTITIES

An important aspect of how identities are created is the difference between avowal and ascribed identities. **Avowal identities** are identities that we choose to associate with and portray. For example, we may reinforce our male or female biological identity through our masculine or feminine clothing, hairstyle, and so on. **Ascribed identities**, on the other hand, are identities that others attribute to us (Fong & Chuang, 2003). For example, when I was in fourth grade, my mother cut my hair really, really short. When we visited an antique shop, the owner called me a "young man." I was devastated! I thought I was *avowing* one identity (female), but I was *ascribed* another identity (male) by this shop owner.

It is important to recognize that whatever your avowed identity, others may ascribe an entirely different identity for you based on what they accept and understand, regardless of how you feel on the matter. Consider Alex, a biological male who has decided he is more comfortable as a woman. She has chosen to avow a female identity by dressing in women's clothing and adopting the female pronoun and a new, female, name. However, others may refuse to accept her avowed identity, and continue to ascribe the male identity to her by continuing to call her Alex, and using the pronoun "he" in reference to her.

MINORITY IDENTITY DEVELOPMENT

As we have seen, we all develop our identities by interacting with other people. However, the stages we go through in this development differ depending on whether we are part of a country's majority or minority identity group (Martin & Nakayama, 2007). While there is some overlap between the two, there are significant differences as well. Let's begin by taking a look at the different stages in minority identity development.

Stage One: Unexamined Identity

Minority identity development begins with **unexamined identity**. This is the stage where an individual doesn't recognize or isn't interested in issues of identity. This is also the point at which individuals who are part of the cultural minority may reject their own culture and embrace the values of the majority culture. At this stage, those who are ethnic minorities may attempt to fit in to the dominant culture, playing down aspects of their own ethnic culture. For example, those who are gay may try to pass as straight, and those who are of a religious minority may shun or play down their traditional practices.

Stage Two: Conformity

The next stage of identity development for minorities is **conformity**. In this stage there is more than an outward visibility of acceptance of the majority culture — there is an adoption and acceptance of the beliefs and values of the dominant culture. People in this stage will openly and vibrantly talk about the majority culture in a positive light, yet talk in a negative manner about themselves and their own culture. For example, people who alter their speech to sound like those in the dominant culture are in the conformity stage of minority identity development. Another example of this is when ethnic or racial minorities refuse to date those outside the dominant culture, based on cultural membership alone.

Stage Three: Resistance and Separatism

The third stage, **resistance and separatism**, is almost 180 degrees different from the conformity stage. Minority group members become disillusioned with the majority group, and not only become distanced from it, but turn their backs on it completely. In going through this stage, group members see the majority group as not just different from their own, but detrimental to themselves and to their culture. For example, someone who is gay may at this point become openly gay in a way that is counter to straight culture. A person of Asian descent in the United States might choose to only have friends who are of Asian descent, and may immerse him- or herself heavily in the history and cultural traditions of his or her ancestry — whether or not these were ever part of life growing up.

Stage Four: Integration

The fourth and final stage of minority identity development is **integration**. In this stage, the individual comes to an understanding that there are positives and negatives in both the majority and minority cultures. They have a solid acceptance of their own culture and value the diversity of the other cultures around them. In this final stage, minority group members are able to appreciate and participate in the traditions and practices of their own culture, yet are also able to appreciate, and perhaps even incorporate, aspects of the majority culture. Consider Eric, a young man who was born in South Korea and was adopted into a white family in New Jersey. Until he was an adolescent, Eric had little interest in his race or his ethnic heritage. Hanging out with his family and friends and playing video games were much more interesting. Gradually, however, Eric became aware of the fact that others perceived him as "Asian," which caused him to be deliberate about proving that he was "American." For example, his parents arranged for the entire family to study the Korean language together and Eric flatly refused to attend classes, noting that he "didn't see the point." In college, however, Eric seemed to go through a transformation. He became interested in Eastern history and culture, he joined the Asian-American students association, he began spending more and more time with his Korean peers, and he (finally) got around to taking those Korean classes. Moreover, he began to feel robbed of the opportunity to grow up in a Korean home. Eventually, however, Eric managed to merge his identities. He is happy and proud to be a member of the family he was raised in and continues to participate in many of the traditions he learned in childhood. But he also continues to enjoy the company of other Korean-Americans and has even joined a Korean-American church. Eric has successfully achieved integration.

Now that we have looked at minority development, let's take a look at how identity development happens in the majority culture, and how that differs from minority identity development.

MAJORITY IDENTITY DEVELOPMENT

Though there are similarities, majority development is different from minority development. In a culture where someone grows up as a member of a majority (whether of race, ethnicity, sexual preference, or so on), the stages of development start out similarly but diverge quickly (Hardiman, 1994). Let's take a deeper look at the different stages in majority identity development.

Stage One: Unexamined Identity

Majority identity development starts out similarly to minority identity development in that the first stage is also **unexamined identity**. However, this stage differs for majority and minority members because while majority members may recognize that differences between cultures exist, they do not yet understand that the majority culture enjoys a privileged position. So, a straight individual in the first stage of development has little understanding that he or she may have certain advantages over those who are gay or bisexual.

Stage Two: Acceptance

In the second stage of development, also known as **acceptance**, majority group members have at least some awareness of the privileges they have over those in minority groups. Some, while they understand that the privilege exists, see this privilege as "the way things are"—unchangeable, or perhaps even natural. For example, someone who is born white in a culture where that is the majority may understand that other races are less privileged, but may feel that nothing can be done about it because it is just the natural order of things.

Others in the majority group may have a deeper understanding of the privilege that they have over minority groups, and believe that such privileges are deserved. For example, an individual may believe that heterosexuality is better than (or more natural than) homosexuality. Someone else might believe that men deserve to have a higher social status than women or that women are to blame for the fact that they often receive less money when they perform the same work as men. They typically hold the view that if there is no change in the status quo, it must be because the minority group wants it that way.

Stage Three: Resistance

Resistance is the next stage in majority development. In this stage, members of the majority group blame themselves for the discrepancies between the majority and minority groups. In this stage, a majority group member may rebel against his or her own group in favor of the minority group. For example, during this stage, members of the white majority experience what some call "white guilt," where they feel that whites are to blame for all aspects of cultural inequality. This stage may or may not be characterized by active resistance against the racism, sexism, or other unearned privilege that they see in their culture.

Stage Four: Redefinition

The fourth stage in majority development is **redefinition**. In this stage, majority group members not only recognize the inequalities between majority and minority groups, but actively fight against their privilege. For example, a man may recognize that a woman in the same position as him at his company is receiving a lesser wage, and instead of feeling that this is simply the status quo and nothing can be done about it (the acceptance stage), he actively campaigns for equal wages for men and women.

Stage Five: Integration

As with minority identity development, **integration** is the final stage of majority identity development. In this stage, people in the majority group understand the privilege that is held by their group and work toward a more equal society. People who have gone through this stage accept and understand their own privilege, and have a greater understanding and appreciation for the minority groups as well.

MULTIRACIAL AND MULTIETHNIC IDENTITY DEVELOPMENT

People who are biracial or multiracial have different identity formations from those who identify with one majority or minority culture (Root, 1990). Miller (1992) argues that biracial children's development is heavily influenced by context. Depending on the racial and cultural makeup of his or her neighborhood and extended family, a biracial child may be socialized more toward one race than another if he or she is frequently surrounded by others of that race and customs associated with a particular ethnicity. On the other hand, the child raised by "both parents in a multiracial community may be socialized towards (being a multiracial individual)," meaning that the child may come to identify with both or all races represented in the family and community (p. 32).

In addition to how their parents choose to raise them, Wallace (2004) points out that a person's physical characteristics can influence their identity development. For example, I have biracial children, but they are rather light skinned. Living in a small town in Wisconsin, there are few Latinos in or near our neighborhood. When my children tell their elementary school classmates they're Latina, their classmates counter, "No, you're white." My children offer their more obviously Latino father as proof, but this does not always sway their classmates who mark light skin as "white."

Though there have been models put forward to describe bi/multiracial identity development, many theorists studying multiracial identity generally agree that its development is less linear than identity development in single-race individuals. There is no specific movement from one stage to another. In fact, even my twin girls, who are racially identical and who were raised in the same community, may differ greatly in their identity formation when it comes to race.

Maria Root (1990) offers five different possibilities for multiracial identity development:

1. **Accept the identity assigned by society.** Obviously this option works best with people who are generally assumed to be one race/ethnicity by society, rather than someone who is more ambiguous and therefore continually questioned about their identity.

2. **Identify actively with both racial groups.** While this may sound like the "easy" solution, it isn't. Often, people who choose this course need to actively and continually construct their identity. They are frequently questioned/challenged about their "choice" of identity. For example, in the movie Selena, Abraham Quintenilla, Selena's father, complains that being Mexican American is difficult because neither side fully accepts you. Similarly, when one takes an active stand in identifying with both racial groups, one may never be fully accepted into either.

3. **Identify with a single racial/ethnic group.** This may seem similar to the first scenario, except that the decision of which group to identify with is made by the individual, and not by society.

4. **Identify with a new ethnic group.** In this scenario, the individual chooses to identify with multiracial people. Unlike the second category, where the individual identifies with both racial groups, here the person identifies more readily with others who are multiracial—regardless of what their various race/ethnicities might be.

5. **Identify symbolically.** In this situation, people of multiracial or multi-ethnic backgrounds who have a very small or distant connection to all but one race or ethnicity may choose to live their day-to-day lives as part of only that race or ethnicity. So, for example, while Laura is one-quarter Puerto Rican and three-quarters Chinese, she lives her everyday life as a Chinese American because that is how she has been raised. She is aware of her Puerto Rican background, but it is incidental in her life.

STEREOTYPES, PREJUDICE, DISCRIMINATION, AND "ISMS"

In a discussion about identity and identity development, topics like stereotypes, prejudice, discrimination, racism, sexism, and so on inevitably come up. It is important to understand the differences between these terms, because they are frequently confused.

- **Stereotypes** are specific generalizations about a group of people that can be positive or negative. A stereotype tells us what other people are like. For instance, you might believe a stereotype that girls like to wear dresses. While this may seem like "natural" knowledge to you, it is actually a culturally conditioned belief. Such a belief may be deeply embedded in a culture.

- **Prejudices** are beliefs or attitudes about a group of people, based on little or no evidence. Prejudices are usually negative. So, whereas stereotypes tell us what people are like, a prejudice describes how we think or feel about a group of people.

- **Discrimination** is an action. When we *act* upon negative beliefs or feelings about a group of people, we are practicing discrimination.

- **The "isms,"** like racism, sexism, ableism, and others, are acts of discrimination directed at a specific group. So, for instance, **racism** is an act of discrimination aimed at a particular racial group; **sexism** is discrimination toward a particular sex or gender, and so on. Many scholars, however, go further in their definition of racism. Some theorists, like Beverly Tatum (2002) and Judy Katz (2003), will tie racism in with cultural power, arguing that racism can only be committed by groups who have cultural power against people who don't. This argument stems from the concept of institutional racism, a form of racism that isn't just committed by individuals, but is supported by institutions as well (Fine, Burns, & Pruitt, 2004). The PBS series *Race—The Power of an Illusion* gives a great example of institutional racism in its discussion of "redlining," the practice of denying home loans to minority groups by deeming them a financial risk. This practice helps to create the wealth gap in the United States, which then further perpetuates the stereotype that people of color are unstable and poor. This understanding of racism as an act of discrimination committed against the minority by the majority can be applied to any of the other commonly understood "isms."

SO — WHO ARE YOU?

Identity is an integral part of intercultural communication. Who we understand ourselves, and others, to be makes an incredible difference in how we communicate with people. Whether we understand someone to be of a particular race, ethnicity, gender, sexual orientation, or religion affects how we talk with them or about them, or whether or not we even speak to them at all. However, as we have also seen, identity is not a static, visible thing that can be touched. Identity is a fluid, changing process that does not depend on biology. It is influenced by our own thoughts and beliefs, our families and friends, our communities, and the media. Identity changes as we grow and interact with other people. Though models of identity development have been created, it is important to understand that no one goes through these models the same way. Some people may remain in the unexamined stage their entire life. Some may progress through some of the stages and then stop. Others may progress through some stages and then regress back into earlier stages. Others may continue this forward-backward pattern through the stages several times throughout their identity development. Also, as I mentioned above, people of multiracial backgrounds can go through completely different models of identity development — perhaps several times. As we proceed to the next chapter to look at intercultural communication in various contexts, remember that how we understand our own and others' identities is a significant factor in those various contexts.

REFERENCES

Bhatia, S. (2007). *American karma: Race, culture, and identity in the Indian diaspora.* New York: New York University Press.

Burke, K. (1966). *Language as symbolic action.* Berkeley: University of California Press.

Cooley, C. H. (1922). *Human nature and the social order* (Rev. ed.). New York: Charles Scribner's Sons.

Fine, M., Burns, A., & Pruitt, L. P. (Eds.). (2004). *Off white: Readings on power, privilege, and resistance.* New York: Routledge.

Fong, M., & Chuang, R. (2003). *Communicating ethnic and cultural identity.* Lonham, MD: Rowman & Littlefield.

Hardiman, R. (1994). White racial identity development in the United States. In E. P. Salett & D. R. Koslow (Eds.), *Race, ethnicity, and self: Identity in multicultural perspective* (pp. 117–140). Washington, DC: National MultiCultural Institute.

Katz, J. H. (2003). *White awareness: Handbook for anti-racism training.* Norman: University of Oklahoma Press.

Martin, J. N., & Nakayama, T. (2007). *Intercultural communication in contexts* (4th ed.). Boston: McGraw-Hill.

Mead, G. H. (1934). *Mind, self and society: From the standpoint of a social behaviorist.* Chicago, IL: University of Chicago Press.

Miller, R. L. (1992). The human ecology of multiracial identity. In M. P. P. Root (Ed.), *Racially mixed people in America* (pp. 24–36). Newbury Park, CA: Sage.

Root, M. P. P. (1990). Resolving "other" status: Identity development of biracial individuals. In L. Brown and M. P. P. Root (Eds.), *Diversity and complexity in feminist therapy* (pp. 185–205). New York: Haworth.

Tatum, B. D. (2002). *Why are all the black kids sitting together in the cafeteria?: And other conversations about race.* New York: Basic Books.

Wallace, K. R. (2004). *Working with multiracial students: Critical perspectives on research and practice.* Charlotte, NC: Information Age Publishing.

4 Borders, Transitions, and Intercultural Communication

When introduced to the concept of borders and transitions in intercultural communication, many students immediately think this refers to traveling to, or studying abroad in, other countries. However, travel across geographic borders is only a part of this topic. **Cultural borders**, borders that are not necessarily designated by geography, but are places where we encounter cultural differences in our everyday lives, are also a crucial part of this study. In this chapter we look at the differences and similarities between geographical borders and cultural borders, discuss the idea of moving across or between borders and culture shock, and examine the not-so-visible cultural borders we live with, and interact with, every day.

TYPES OF BORDERS

It is important to note that crossing a geographical border does not mean automatically encountering a different cultural landscape, nor do cultural borders necessarily fall along geographical lines, but of course in some cases they do overlap. We further define the two types of borders below and examine the visibility, and invisibility, of both geographic and cultural borders.

GEOGRAPHIC BORDERS

Geographic borders separate one area of land from another, and are determined by people. Some of these boundaries are easily identifiable and visible, such as state lines and national borders, but others, like county or town lines, are less so. If you live in the United States, think quickly — do you know where your county lines are? It's very likely you don't. Very few people can identify their own county borders because these borders don't generally have a huge impact on their everyday lives. State lines are a bit more obvious in the United States, but even those can become invisible for some people. For example, my mother lived on the eastern part of the United States, and would cross two states in her commute to work every morning without even thinking. On the other hand, my family and I live in Wisconsin, very close to the Minnesota border, and we often travel to the town right on the other side of the border. Although it is only a fifteen-minute drive, my daughters always complain "We have to go all the way to Minnesota today!" To them, state lines are a noticeable demarcation (reinforced by the large "Welcome to Minnesota" sign that greets them upon our arrival), thus making the quick trip feel like a significant journey. Of course, if you have to board a plane in order to cross state lines, it feels like even more of a journey and makes that border even more noticeable to you.

National borders seem even more significant in no small part due to the many requirements for crossing them, like procuring a visa, passing through immigration, and going through customs. However, more than the length of the trip or the motions we go through, the cultural differences we expect to see when we cross a national border are what make the crossing so significant. We expect changes in language, changes in cultural norms, and changes in the everyday understandings of life. Certainly, in many cases, cultural borders coincide with national borders. However, what we often don't see, or don't recognize, are those cultural borders that are not as easily identified.

CULTURAL BORDERS

As I defined at the beginning of this chapter, the places where we face cultural differences are known as cultural borders. So, where might we find these cultural borders? Certainly they exist along other, less prominent geographic borders, like between towns, neighborhoods, or even between streets within a neighborhood. For example, my editor, who is Chinese American, lives in Brooklyn, New York, and the street she lives on has a fairly mixed demographic. However, the next street over is inhabited by a predominantly Orthodox Jewish community, whose cultural practices, like their dress and their language, are quite different from her own. Therefore, for her, turning the corner onto the next street also means crossing a cultural border.

It is also important to recognize that cultural borders can exist separate from geographic borders, that they are not physical borders, and that they can exist between individuals. As I explained in Chapter 1, our names, our skin color, our food preferences, are all cultural. Individually, these aspects may have little meaning, but together, they become markers of our identity and our cultural borders. However, it is important to recognize that we don't each have a cultural border around us at all times, and that our cultural borders are relative to the person we are interacting with. The definition of a cultural border is a place where you encounter cultural difference, so therefore, if you are interacting with someone who identifies as the same race as you, you may not feel a cultural boundary exists on that front. Of course, if that person identifies with a different sexual orientation than you, you may experience a cultural border there. A way to visualize this is to think of a Venn diagram: some aspects of your identity will overlap with the person or group of people you are interacting with and some aspects of your identity will not.

While we are able to easily recognize others' cultural differences, we are less able to recognize our own. Our own cultural borders appear invisible to us because we are so embedded in our own cultures that our behaviors simply seem "normal" to us. We generally don't notice our cultural borders until we see the reaction others have when they encounter them. Even when we do notice a difference, we have a tendency to assume that the difference is on the part of the other person, rather than understand that they are encountering our cultural border. Consider Angela, who has lived in Boston all her life. To her, "iced tea" means unsweetened tea with ice cubes and a few slices of lemon in it. When an exchange student from Hong Kong, Carina, comes to stay with Angela's family, she is surprised to discover that the iced tea has lemon in it and not milk and sugar. Angela simply tells Carina that iced tea is always made with lemon, brushing aside any notion that "iced tea" might be a different beverage elsewhere. This assumption reinforces the belief that the practices and behaviors we are accustomed to are "normal," and presumes that difference exists only in others. However, as a student of intercultural communication, it is important to challenge that assumption and be aware that you, too, have cultural borders that others will encounter and interact with. Whether you encounter someone else's cultural border, or they encounter yours, you should never assume that anything is "normal"; any differences you, or others, encounter, are simply that: different, not "weird" or "wrong."

ENCOUNTERING BORDERS AND CULTURE SHOCK

When people are aware that they are interacting with or crossing a cultural border, they expect to encounter differences in many of aspects of everyday life, like food, language, daily customs, and ways of thinking. However, interacting with cultural borders can still be a difficult, shocking, and sometimes even alienating experience because the stable ground of "normalcy" that we take for granted suddenly shifts. In this section, I discuss what it means to "collide" with a border, and I also examine culture shock and the various models associated with this concept.

COLLIDING WITH BORDERS

For the most part, when people encounter a cultural border, they choose to cross it to some degree, whether that means trying a new food, or picking up bits of a different language, or learning about a religion different from their own. However, in some cases, when people recognize a cultural border, they collide into it instead of crossing it. I use the term "collide" figuratively, because while there is no physical barrier present, the reaction people have when colliding into a cultural border can be similar to that of someone running into a wall. A great example of this is seen in a study I conducted of a bar that held a weekly event called "Latino Night" (Willis, 1997). While the midwestern college town where this bar was located was predominately white, over one hundred people, 90 precent of them Latino, would gather at this bar once a week to enjoy the Spanish-language music being played, and dance. One of the things I observed and studied was the reactions of non-Latinos when they entered the bar. Due to the fact that there were no signs outside the bar indicating it was "Latino Night," white patrons would walk into the bar and collide with the cultural border established by the difference in music and physical appearance of the patrons from "the usual." Upon entering, they would spring back a bit, and linger around the door with surprised looks on their faces. In most cases, they would ask the bouncer what was going on, and when the bouncer told them it was "Latino Night," they would nod and leave.

This example shows that some people choose not to engage with a cultural border. They collide into it, acknowledge it, and then turn away from it. However, even if a person eventually chooses to interact with, or cross, a border, that initial "collision" moment might still occur. We are generally so absorbed and used to our everyday routine, that when we do encounter something different—be it a difference in language, in religion, in political views—we are caught off guard.

CULTURE SHOCK

Intercultural scholars refer to our feelings of surprise and distress when we cross a cultural border as **culture shock**, which is a "relatively short-term feeling of disorientation, of discomfort due to the unfamiliarity of surroundings and the lack of familiar cues in the environment" (Martin & Nakayama, 2007, p. 310). Culture shock is a feeling that many people go through when entering new surroundings and interacting with people from cultures different from their own. The key words here are "new" and "different"—when we are surrounded by environments or people similar to us we don't feel culture shock. For example, an American tourist traveling to Cabo San Lucas in Mexico and staying at a tourist resort is highly unlikely to feel culture shock. The tourist district of Cabo San Lucas is designed to cater to people from the United States, and many of the people who work there are trained very specifically in the culture and customs of the United States to make American tourists feel as comfortable and the surroundings as familiar as possible. However, if the same American tourist were to wander outside of the tourist district into more "local" areas, he or she might very well experience culture shock.

Scholars have developed two models that chart the progress of a person's experience of culture shock: the u-curve model and the w-curve model. We now take a look at both, as well as variations on those models.

The U-Curve Model

First introduced by Lysgaard in 1955, the **u-curve model** describes how travelers go through various stages of cultural adjustment, starting off on a high note, then going down into culture shock and periods of despair, and finally going back up into cultural adjustment and/or adaptation. Oberg (1960) expands on Lysgaard's original idea and details four stages of adjustment to a new culture in the u-curve model:

1. **The "honeymoon" stage.** In this first stage, the traveler is caught up in the wonder, excitement, and novelty of the culture. While everything does seem strange, it is strange in a new and exciting way.

2. **The hostility stage.** At this point, travelers realize that they have to live with their new situation on a day-to-day basis and give up much of what was familiar to them, like what they eat for breakfast, what they watch on television, and how they travel to and from places. Due to the loss of familiarity and comfort, a feeling of hostility toward their host culture can emerge in travelers. They might turn against their host, express this hostility by embracing stereotypes, and spend more time with fellow travelers from their same home culture, rather than meeting new people from their host culture. Behaviors like these can foster an "us vs. them" attitude in the traveler.

3. **The recovery stage.** In this third stage, travelers are able to come to a new appreciation for their host culture, because they have become increasingly familiar and comfortable with their surroundings, including the language, customs, and everyday understandings.

4. **The acceptance stage.** This is the final stage, where the traveler is completely accustomed to and fully integrated into the host culture.

Reentry Shock and the W-Curve Model

Many intercultural scholars argue that the u-curve model is missing a crucial aspect of culture shock: **reentry shock**. The temporal, psychological difficulties involved are similar to those of culture shock, but this occurs when a traveler returns to his or her home culture after having lived in the host culture for a significant time. In fact, many travelers report that reentry shock is worse than the original culture shock they experienced in their host culture (Uehara, 1986). Reentry shock often is worse because travelers don't expect it; they assume that because they are returning to where they originally came from, they will already be used to what it's like there. However, because travelers have been exposed to new ideas and customs in their host culture, they return home with new views and ideas, while those who stayed at home remain the same. Also, travelers often have a changed perspective on their previous life; not only do their old ways not seem "normal" anymore, they often can't understand why no one else questions what is done in their everyday lives. They may feel few people from their home culture are able to understand their new perspective, leading to feelings of isolation and dissonance.

This understanding of the reentry experience resulted in scholars developing the **w-curve model**, which begins in the same way as the u-curve model, but then repeats itself to show a similar experience upon reentry. That is, the model shows the traveler going through the stages outlined in the u-curve model—the honeymoon stage, the hostility stage, the recovery stage, and the acceptance stage—when they arrive in the new culture, and repeating those same stages when they return home (Gullahorn & Gullahorn, 1963).

There are a few important things to understand about both of these models of transition. First, the models reflect the general patterns of culture shock and reentry shock, but not all people go through these transitions the same way. Some people may feel very little reentry or culture shock; others may feel a great deal. Some people will go through these stages very quickly, others will take months or years to go through each stage. Some people will never even get through the stages at all, choosing instead to stay with their own compatriots and seclude themselves from their host culture, or to leave their host culture before the recovery stage and return home.

Also, it is important to understand that movement through the stages of these models is not necessarily linear or continuous. While it might appear from sketches or descriptions of the models that a traveler would move down from the honeymoon stage into the hostility stage and back up to the recovery stage and acceptance stage, this linear progression (or digression) may not be what actually happens. In reality, there are various ups and downs in this progress: a person may arrive at a new culture experiencing the full honeymoon stage, then be hit with an experience that may drive him or her toward the hostility stage, and then have another experience where they are brought back to the honeymoon stage. This up-and-down movement may continue, with the movement generally going down toward culture shock, and then back up toward readjustment, both in the first and second phases of the w-curve model.

CULTURAL OTHERS AT HOME

We expect to interact with people who differ culturally from us when traveling abroad, but what about at home? When we think of cultural others at home, the first group of people that may come to mind are immigrants. Immigrants can be either voluntary or involuntary: **voluntary immigrants** migrate of their own free will, whereas **involuntary immigrants** are forced either by people or circumstances to leave their home countries. For example, some involuntary refugees must flee their home countries because of political infighting, genocide, or other problems. Some involuntary immigrants are taken from their homes forcibly. The clearest example of this is slavery. Many groups of people that arrived originally as slaves have become part of the fabric of the country to which they were brought, like African Americans in the United States, many of whom are descended from slave populations stolen from West African and Caribbean countries from the 1600s until the Civil War.

Many people think of slavery as something that happened long ago, but slavery does still occur all over the world. **Human trafficking** is a form of modern-day slavery, and is defined by the International Labor Organization as "the recruitment, transportation, transfer, harboring or receipt of persons, by means of the threat or use of force or other forms of coercion, of abduction, of fraud, of deception, of the abuse of power or of a position of vulnerability or of the giving or receiving of payments or benefits to achieve the consent of a person having control over another person, for the purpose of exploitation" (United Nations, 2000, p. 2). According to U.S. government-sponsored research done in 2006, it is estimated that approximately 800,000 people are taken involuntarily across national borders each year (U.S. State Department, 2008).

How immigrants and the host culture interact with each other can have significant implications for intercultural communication. We now take a look at the interaction between the two groups from both the perspective of the immigrant and the perspective of the host culture.

THE IMMIGRANT'S PERSPECTIVE

Whether they migrate to a new country by choice or by force, all immigrants must reconcile the cultural behaviors they were used to in their home country with their new environment and the cultural behaviors of the host country. How they do so can be generalized into four categories: **assimilation, separation, integration,** and **marginalization** (Berry, 2003).

1. **Assimilation** is where the immigrant completely adopts the host culture as his or her own. He or she follows the traditions, norms, and cultural understandings of the host culture, abandoning the culture of the home country. An immigrant who has assimilated uses the language of the host culture, striving to perfect language skills. The immigrant adopts the food, cultural greetings, celebrations, and everyday understandings of the host culture.

2. **Separation** is the exact opposite of assimilation; the immigrant completely rejects (as much as possible) the host culture and any overtures to join it. Immigrants who take this path strive to keep their own language, customs, and understandings. They may choose to live in areas where there is a high concentration of similar immigrants. In many places throughout the world, immigrants can live in host countries without a drastic need to adopt or adapt to the host culture. For example, there are many ethnic neighborhoods, like Chinatown or Little Italy, across the United States where immigrants can speak, eat, and interact in much the same way that they did in their home country because they are surrounded by immigrants from the same culture.

3. **Integration** is a blend of assimilation and separation. Immigrants who integrate adopt aspects of the host culture while retaining some aspects

of their home cultures. For example, they may strive to learn the language of their host culture, but retain some of the celebrations and food choices from their home culture. They may work to have their children grow up bilingual, that is, speak the language of both the home culture and the host culture.

4. **Marginalization** is characterized by an immigrant's desire for integration that is rejected by the host culture. The host culture may reject the immigrant's use of the host language because of an accent, or reject the immigrant because she or he doesn't "look" like a native. Though the immigrant may try to become a part of the host culture, she or he is kept on the margins.

THE HOST CULTURE'S PERSPECTIVE

In general, host countries do recognize the need to help immigrants acclimate to their new environment, and try to make them feel included and welcome. Most countries, especially those that have a high concentration of immigrants, have resources and the infrastructure in place to help immigrants assimilate to their new culture, especially at the institutional level. For example, the U.S. Equal Employment Opportunity Commission works against discrimination based on national origin. In many places in New York and California where Hispanic immigrants settle, advertisements for legal services and government notices are written in both Spanish and English, so immigrants who have limited English can still access government or legal aid. Also, in most polling areas during elections, translators for various languages are on hand to help immigrants understand the ballot, so they can fully exercise their right to vote. In Hong Kong, after the influx of immigrants from mainland China since the 1997 handover, the subway announcements started to be made in both Cantonese (the dialect of Chinese spoken in Hong Kong) and Mandarin (the dialect spoken by most mainland Chinese).

However, this is not to say there is never any hostility toward immigrants from members of the host culture. This hostility is not necessarily open, but the stereotypes or assumptions the host culture has about immigrants can manifest themselves in small, but meaningful, ways. For example, there is a general assumption made by some members of the dominant culture in the United States that immigrants, particularly Latino immigrants, are coming and "stealing" their jobs and resources. How this stereotype of Latino immigrants as "untrustworthy" is reflected in our daily lives was evident during a shopping trip I made to a JCPenney store in Ohio. While I was waiting in line to pay, I noticed a sign written in Spanish that had a picture of an angel on it with a big splotch in the middle of her gown, which warned customers that the security tags on clothing would ruin the garment with ink if the tag were forcibly removed. This was the only sign in the store written in Spanish, and there was no English equivalent. What message does this send to Spanish-speaking people in the United States? Certainly not an inclusive one! You can imagine that Latinos, immigrants or not, recognizing the underlying message of the sign would feel alienated and like second-class citizens, which could, in turn, result in their own dismissal of the host culture.

It is important to recognize the assumptions and stereotypes we have about others, and see the discrimination that exists not only on an institutional level, but also on an everyday level, so that communication between cultural others and the host culture doesn't shut down.

BORDER CULTURE

In previous sections of this chapter, we've discussed the differences encountered when crossing cultural borders, whether or not they coincide with geographic borders. However, it is also important for intercultural scholars to look at the geographic border itself, which often has its own unique cultural space and a different cultural identity from the areas on either side of the border (Anzaldúa, 1999). Think about it: when you travel, you don't immediately step into a new culture the minute you step over a border. Language, especially on official signs, may change, and the monetary system may change, but there is a degree of fluidity—it isn't necessarily an abrupt and rigid change. For example, businesses on the Mexican side of the U.S.–Mexico border might welcome American dollars, and proprietors have most likely learned to speak some English to accommodate travelers from the United States. Those who live on or near a geographic border have a lived understanding of how both cultures work and function, and often border culture is a hybrid of the cultures of the two sides it separates (Anzaldúa, 1999).

You can see examples of this hybridity in the language used in geographic borders or places near geographic borders. If the geographic border separates two cultural areas that speak two different languages, bilingual signs and public announcements are typically the norm, and in some cases the border culture even develops a **pidgin language**, a simplified and unifying language that is created by melding the two different languages. Language is not the only hybrid aspect of these border cultures: a mix of the important holidays and everyday customs from both sides of the border is practiced in the space of the border. However, this blending of cultures in the space of the border can be a difficult and frustrating thing for the people who live there.

Drawing from her own experience, Gloria Anzaldúa writes of *una abierta herida,* an open wound, that "grates against the third world and bleeds," in her book *Borderlands = La Frontera* (1999). The "third world" she writes about is the border space between the United States and Mexico where she lived, and the reason she refers to it as an open wound is because that border represents an area where the cultures of the United States and Mexico are forced to coexist, and not in a peaceful way. There can be no equal and harmonious blend of the two cultures, because the dynamic of majority vs. minority culture exists, and one culture's behaviors or customs are valued more. Certainly this dynamic alone can cause problems, but power shifts and population changes mean that the border's culture is tenuous and constantly redefining itself, which is painful, as far as identity, for those who live there. Imagine being part of a culture that is an ever-changing mix of two cultures: you might feel as though you belong to both and to neither simultaneously.

REFERENCES

Anzaldúa, G. (1999). *Borderlands = La frontera.* San Francisco: Aunt Lute Books.

Berry, J. W. (2003). Conceptual approaches to acculturation. In K. M. Chun, P. B. Organista, & G. Marin (Eds.), *Acculturation: Advances in theory, measurement, and applied research.* Washington, DC: American Psychological Association.

Gullahorn, J. T., & Gullahorn, J. E. (1963). An extension of the u-curve hypothesis. *Journal of Social Science, 19*(3), 33–47.

Lysgaard, S. (1955). Adjustment in a foreign society: Norwegian Fulbright grantees visiting the United States. *International Social Science Bulletin, 7,* 45–51.

Martin, J. N., & Nakayama, T. K. (2007). *Intercultural communication in contexts* (4th ed.). Boston: McGraw-Hill.

Oberg, K. (1960). Cultural shock: Adjustment to new cultural environments. *Practical Anthropology, 7,* 177–182.

Uehara, A. (1986). The nature of American student reentry adjustment and perceptions of the sojourn experience. *International Journal of Intercultural Relations, 10,* 415–438.

United Nations. (2000). *Protocol to prevent, suppress and punish trafficking in persons, especially women and children, supplementing the United Nations convention against transnational organized crime.* Retrieved from http://untreaty.un.org/English/TreatyEvent2003/Texts/treaty2E.pdf

U.S. State Department. (2008, June). *Trafficking in persons report.* Retrieved from http://www.state.gov/documents/organization/105655.pdf

Willis, J. L. (1997). Latino night: Performances of a Latino/a culture in northwest Ohio. *Communication Quarterly, 45,* 335–354.

5 Intercultural Communication in Context: Relationships and Organizations

In previous chapters, we looked at a few of the basic concepts in intercultural communication: definitions of culture, verbal and nonverbal communication, identity development, and cultural borders. In this chapter, we take those basic concepts and examine how intercultural communication impacts two important contexts: relationships and organizations.

INTERCULTURAL COMMUNICATION AND RELATIONSHIPS

In its broadest definition, an **intercultural relationship** occurs when two people of different cultural backgrounds come together in a mutual connection. When you hear the word "relationship," you may automatically think of a romantic relationship. And while intercultural marriages and partnerships certainly are an important example of intercultural relationships, they are not the only ones; friendships, business relationships, and family relationships can also be intercultural in nature. In the sections that follow, we look at a number of different facets of intercultural relationships, including bounded and dominant relationships, interracial relationships, and, finally, the benefits and challenges of interracial relationships.

BOUNDED AND DOMINANT INTERCULTURAL RELATIONSHIPS

My parents enjoy a happy intercultural relationship. My mother is of French and English descent and my father's family is Italian and English. My mother most closely identifies with her French heritage, my father with his English heritage. These are my parents' *bounded identities* — aspects of identity that matter to an individual but may not be recognized by the world at large. (Compare bounded identities to the avowed identities discussed in Chapter 3.) My parents have a **bounded intercultural relationship**, or a relationship with cultural differences defined by the individuals involved although these differences may not be recognized by others. Why don't others see the differences? Well, my parents experienced personal differences based on culture that needed to be negotiated in their marriage — food preferences, holiday celebrations, and so on. However, other people can sometimes view these differences as unimportant. After all, my parents are both white, they share the same religious beliefs, they both speak unaccented American English, and they both grew up in the United States.

Dominant intercultural relationships, on the other hand, are relationships with cultural differences that are readily recognized by society. For example, the marriage of a black man from Jamaica to a white woman from Norway would form a dominant intercultural relationship, as would the close friendship between a Chinese American Catholic woman and a white Jewish woman. The differences between these relational partners are quite obvious and salient and, therefore, dominant. (Compare dominant identity with ascribed identity discussed in Chapter 3.) Thus, these partners are easily identified as "culturally different," while bounded intercultural couples are assumed to be "culturally similar," despite differences that matter to the relational partners. The key difference here is visibility or how apparent the differences between the partners are. This can mean anything that is physically obvious, such as skin color, religion (reflected, for example, by wearing a yarmulke), physical ability, differences in age, and so on.

Not surprisingly, intercultural relationships with dominant differences are treated generally differently from bounded intercultural relationships—particularly when the relationship consists of a majority group member and a minority group member (say, a white man married to a Latina woman). Based on the reactions of the people around them, the white man may see and experience prejudice for the first time because the inequality that minority cultures face may be extended to him via his partner. This can be frustrating, at best, and may even cause a paradigm shift for the majority group member, causing him to move from one stage of majority identity development to another. In other words, if our fictional Caucasian man recognizes prejudice for the first time when spending time with his minority group member wife, he might move from stage two (acceptance) to stage three (resistance).

INTERRACIAL RELATIONSHIPS

As mentioned above, interracial relationships are particularly visible examples of intercultural relationships. They also have a long and complicated history in the United States. Until June of 1967, interracial marriages were outlawed in many parts of the nation (the Supreme Court case *Loving vs. Virginia* finally made interracial marriage legal). Since then, legal unions between individuals of different races have grown exponentially. In 2000, 6 percent of all marriages in the United States were interracial marriages or involved partners of different origins, an increase of nearly fourfold since 1970 (U.S. Census Bureau, 2003). However, even this statistic may fail to reflect the number of interracial partners, as the government only records information about married couples. Interracial couples who cohabitate and interracial committed gay and lesbian couples are largely ignored in this data. In addition, the government may categorize or define race differently than the individuals involved in interracial relationships. For example, a woman from a Korean background and a man from an Indian background would be considered a same-race couple by the government because both individuals are "Asian." However, given the vast differences between Korean and Indian culture and the visibly different appearances of people from these cultures, it is likely that the couple would perceive themselves and be perceived as interracial. The United States government also fails to recognize people of Hispanic/Latino descent as a race (Latino is considered an ethnicity, as we learned in Chapter 3). Therefore a Latino/Caucasian couple like my husband and I cannot register as an interracial couple.

THE BENEFITS AND CHALLENGES OF INTERCULTURAL RELATIONSHIPS

Whether or not interracial relationships are regarded as such, there are many benefits — and many challenges — that come along with them. For example, there is simply no better way to experience another culture than to have close contact with its members. You can read all you want about holidays associated with Islam or Christianity or traditional foods from India and Italy, but it is not the same as engaging with those cultures via a colleague, a friend, or a romantic partner. These relationships give us the chance to learn about differences in cultural meanings, values, and communication, thereby gaining a much deeper and perspective-broadening understanding of another culture.

In addition, intercultural relationships offer relational partners (majority group relational partners in particular) the opportunity to see the world through another's eyes, especially where stereotyping and prejudice are concerned. For example, I once had a student who shared with the class that he would get frustrated when he heard minority group members "play the race card" during political discussions. Then, as a freshman in college, he became close friends with an African American student in his dorm. One day, they were at the mall in a record store (back in the days when people actually purchased CDs!) and my student was troubled to find a salesclerk following him and his friend around. He assumed that the clerk wanted to pounce on them to make a sale, but his friend said: "This always happens to me. It's because I'm a young, black, male." My student had gotten harassed by one store clerk on one occasion. What he gained from that experience was an appreciation for what it might be like to experience such frustration regularly. Other examples are equally valid here: If a person spent time with his or her elderly grandmother, he or she might be surprised to see how disrespectfully many individuals speak to older Americans. Our culture values youth and vitality, so elderly people are seen as feeble, weak, and slow. These new understandings allow for changing attitudes, and perhaps even a desire to fight unearned privilege based on majority race, religion, age, and so on.

Despite the clear benefits of intercultural relationships, we must not ignore the challenges that they bring, particularly when that intercultural relationship is highly visible to the rest of society. Individuals in these relationships may face continuous questioning from friends and family about the viability and/or the wisdom of the relationship, and they may find that their relationship becomes an open forum for public debate. For example, in the movie *Bend It Like Beckham* (2002), Jess, an Indian girl living in London, begins to fall for her white Irish soccer coach. When her sister finds out, she cautions her not to take her crush too far because she wouldn't want her to be "the one that everyone stares at . . . because [she] married the English bloke." In a romantic intercultural relationship there are often questions about the potential children from the union — questions about whether they will have a confused identity or perhaps even a less-privileged one. Like the example from *Bend It Like Beckham* above, an intercultural couple may face disapproval from both of their families and others that belong to the same culture for not dating or marrying within their particular group. All of these pressures can cause people involved in a relationship to question themselves, or try to conceive of their own cultural identity within the relationship in a new and different way. Therefore, a Christian Asian man in a friendship with a nonreligious white man may find himself being pulled away by friends in his own cultural group, not necessarily out of hostility, but because of perceived pressure to remain loyal to his own group.

Other intercultural relational partners may not receive such verbally direct pressure to end or reconsider their friendship or romantic relationships, but may instead receive more subtle nonverbal indications of disapproval. They may find that people stare, point, or avoid making eye contact with them when they are in public. For example, a married couple with a considerable age gap may find people staring or even snickering outright when they walk down the street hand in hand.

MISUNDERSTANDINGS IN INTERCULTURAL RELATIONSHIPS

I would be remiss if I didn't bring up an important aspect of intercultural communication that is largely ignored in general discussions of intercultural relationships: culturally derived definitions leading to misunderstandings between relational partners from different cultures. What does this mean? Consider the following questions: What does it mean to be a friend? What does it mean to date? What does it mean to "be in love"? Your answers to these questions will largely depend on your cultural background, or at least on the most salient and important parts of your culture with which you identify. For example, in the United States, we tend to have a number of people we refer to as "friends" — perhaps even hundreds of people that we are "friends" with via social networking tools like Facebook. But we likely only have a handful of people that we consider "good friends," and even fewer who are "close friends" or "lifelong friends" with whom we share the most intimate details of our lives. In other cultures, however, there may not be a clear-cut distinction between "close friends" and "friends," and these differing assumptions about levels of friendship can lead to misunderstandings. Imagine you are chatting with someone of a different culture whom you consider to be a casual friend. Suddenly, this person begins to ask you some personal questions and you become uncomfortable. In your mind, this person had no right to ask such personal questions; in your friend's mind, such questions are fair game with anyone who achieves the status of "friend."

This same issue may exist in intercultural romantic relationships, as different cultures have different understandings of what it means to "date" or be "in love." Some cultures, such as many cultures in India, still have arranged marriages; other cultures believe that dating should exist for the sole purpose of finding a life partner (this is sometimes called courting). Still other cultures, such as the United States, encourage individuals to date widely in order to experience many types of relationships. Clearly such differing definitions can cause misunderstandings, not to mention hurt feelings or dashed expectations. For example, as a graduate student I would sometimes go to "Latino Night" at a club near my campus as I greatly enjoyed some of the live musical performances. Often I would be asked to dance by Latino men — mostly men I hadn't met or been introduced to. In the culture I grew up in, if a man asks a woman to dance, he most often has an interest in dating her. So I was often confused when the song ended and my dance partner escorted me back to my seat without any type of conversation or follow-up. It took me quite some time to understand and accept that these men were simply seeking someone to dance with — they were interested in a five-minute connection with someone who enjoys music, not a lifetime commitment. When we are involved in intercultural relationships, we are exposed to these additional, alternative ways of understanding the world. While such misunderstandings are a natural part of it, we do learn to broaden our horizons and reflect on our own definitions of ideas and concepts, which we often take for granted as "the norm."

INTERCULTURAL COMMUNICATION AND ORGANIZATIONS

Intercultural communication is not just an important aspect of our everyday relationships, it is also important in organizations. What do I mean by **organizations**? I mean groups with a formal governance and structure including (but not limited to) businesses, governments, educational institutions, religious institutions, and nonprofits. Such groups present the opportunity to work with people, and very often these people represent different religions, races, ethnicities, ages, and so on. In this section we look at how intercultural communication affects organizations, paying special attention to identity and verbal and nonverbal communication.

INTERCULTURAL COMMUNICATION, ORGANIZATIONS, AND IDENTITY

Consider an organization you belong to—perhaps a campus club or your part-time job. What do the other organizational members look like? What do they believe? Where do they come from? Chances are, the people you are working with look very different from the people your parents worked with; and the folks your parents worked with likely looked much different from the individuals your grandparents dealt with in organizations. Times continue to change: Women represented just over 45 percent of the workforce in 1975 and were nearly 60 percent of the U.S. workforce in 2005 (Department of Labor, 2005). There were nearly seventy million people of color in the U.S. population in 2000. If you add in the over 35 million people of Hispanic/Latino descent, that gives us well over 100 million people in the United States who are not white (U.S. Census, 2000); in 1975, people of color comprised only 10 percent of the U.S. population. Accordingly, there has been an increase in the number of people of color in the U.S. workforce over the past thirty years. This rise, however, is not due only to population increases; it is also a result of legal equal opportunity measures that have created accepting and stable work environments for people of various religions, ages, abilities, races, ethnicities, and so on.

All of these important changes in organizations have affected how we interact with others, particularly in the workplace. For example, it used to be entirely acceptable for male colleagues to make jokes about women (particularly blonde women); it was also once acceptable to make comments or derisive remarks about people's race or sexual orientation. Today these jokes are not only considered distasteful and socially unacceptable, but they fit the legal definition of **harassment**, communication that intends to hurt or offend an individual, creating a hostile environment. In addition, organizations are now legally required to accommodate people with differing abilities by such actions as installing wheelchair ramps in new office buildings (U.S. Department of Justice, 1994).

Organizational change also appears in more subtle ways. For example, some school districts have changed their calendars to accommodate not only Christian holidays, but Jewish holidays as well (Anna, 2006). Some schools have changed dress codes that forbade the use of caps and head scarves to allow for religious differences, such as permitting female students to wear a *hijab* (head covering) to school in observance of the Muslim faith. Occasionally, individuals in an organization resist change and argue that the original way is "the way it has always been." Large-scale change can be a frightening thing and it can be challenging to acclimate to new ways of doing things. But when a behavior is systematically unfair to or uncomfortable for others, it is important that it be changed so that organizations welcome everyone.

ORGANIZATIONS AND VERBAL COMMUNICATION

Clearly, organizations must deal with intercultural communication within the group. Yet they must also address intercultural issues when working outside of the group, particularly in the realm of international business. Both within and outside the group, verbal communication is incredibly powerful. Let's take a look at how verbal communication differences play out in an organizational setting when it comes to the language of business as well as the appropriate greetings and politeness.

The Language of Business

One of the first things you might notice about how business is conducted internationally is that transactions between organizations in different countries usually happen in the same language: English. As you may recall from our discussion of verbal communication in Chapter 2, the language we speak affects how we think; our choice of words communicates our cultural values (Smagorinski, 2001). This is especially evident in different cultures' sayings and proverbs. For instance, in the United States time is seen as a valuable commodity not to be wasted, and this belief is reflected in phrases such as "time is money," "the early bird gets the worm," and "no time like the present." You might think that it is "natural" to feel that time should not be wasted and that every moment should be used to the fullest, but — as I have mentioned before — such views are culturally influenced and determined. In sharp contrast, the Guyanan proverb "Yuh can't suck cane and blow whistle" means "Don't try to do two things at once." This is because Guyanese people differ from Americans in their perception of time — and how time should be spent.

If English is the dominant language in international business, then the *values* underlying the English language are the dominant values of global organizations. However, just because such values as the importance of time or technology are conveyed in the English language doesn't mean they automatically translate to nonnative English speakers, even during business transactions. Take the conflicting English and Guyanese sayings about time and trying to do too much at once. Now imagine that Kara, a native English speaker, is trying to impress upon her Guyanese boss, Julie, how important it is to read over the time-sensitive memo she needs to send out to the entire company. Julie, who is busy with another project, says that it needs to wait. Kara is frustrated with the fact that her boss can't appreciate the urgency of her request and can't understand why her boss can't do both tasks at the same time. On the other hand, Julie feels she doesn't have enough energy to focus on both at the same time, and can't understand why Kara is pressing her to hurry up. As you can see, both parties are using the same verbal code (the English language) but this does not necessarily translate into shared cultural values. It is important to be aware of these individual differences in your organization, so that you can be more sensitive and considerate of what others consider important.

Greetings and Politeness

Greetings across cultures are different in that they use different words (for example, *hola* is the Spanish word for "hello"), but are also different in the basic conception of what a greeting is. In the United States, for example, you may greet someone you have just met by saying "Hello! How are you today?" You don't actually expect an answer that involves lots of details about family situations, health problems, or job frustrations. Rather, you expect the person to be very vague: "I'm doing pretty well, thanks." In other cultures, however, such a question may envelop you in a one-hour conversation! In many Asian countries "Have you eaten yet?" is a typical greeting, and in Botswana, you may be asked "How did you wake?" All of these are **greeting scripts**, or understandings for how to meet others in a polite manner.

Politeness is extremely important, especially in international business interactions, which is why many organizations that send their staff abroad offer training on appropriate and polite behavior. For example, a French student once told me that before she and her parents accepted an American study-abroad student to live in their home for a semester, they all attended a seminar on what to expect. They learned, for example, that many Americans shower every day. This is not an attempt to waste water, but rather an important cultural focus on cleanliness. Similarly, in many Asian cultures, it is polite to refuse food at least once or twice when it is offered to you, even if you are very hungry. To accept food the first time it is offered is rude. However, in the United States, if someone offers you food and you refuse, it probably won't be offered to you again. This difference in politeness can be an unintended cause of rudeness (or hunger!).

Organizational meetings can be another place where misunderstandings occur because of differing ideas of what is polite and acceptable behavior. For example, in the United States, most organizational meetings get straight to the point. It is considered respectful for the leader of the meeting to follow a strict agenda and not waste anyone's time with random, off-topic, or even personal conversations (Morrison & Conaway, 2006). This is a common practice in many Western countries. However, in some other countries, it is considered rude to get straight to the point; people from these countries may not feel comfortable doing business with people they do not know and would probably prefer a meeting that begins with small talk and allows them to be introduced to their colleagues. What we might consider "normal" protocol can be a deal breaker in international business.

When we work in organizations, understanding how greetings and politeness function is very important. As we understand intercultural communication more deeply, we can at least be aware of these potential issues, even if we cannot memorize or internalize every politeness ritual of the cultures we are dealing with. The simple acknowledgment that differences exist can prevent frustration and save business relationships.

ORGANIZATIONS AND NONVERBAL COMMUNICATION

As we learned in Chapter 2, verbal communication makes up a large percentage of our communication with others. This is true of nonverbal communication as well—particularly when the verbal code causes confusion (for example, two individuals do not speak the same language). There are many nonverbal behaviors that impact intercultural organizational communication, such as notions of saving face, nonverbal greetings, and even ways of walking in relation to others. However, since I could fill several books on this topic, I must limit myself to a brief overview of two of the more important nonverbal cues: time and space.

Time

When we looked at time earlier, we talked about the importance of time in the United States, which runs on very strict schedules, and where being "on time" is considered important. I often ask students to think about having a ten o'clock appointment in a few different contexts. For example, I ask them what time they would arrive if their ten o'clock appointment were a class. They generally respond, "A few minutes before ten." When I ask them how they would feel if they arrived twenty minutes late for class, most students say that they wouldn't bother showing up—it would be embarrassing and rude to walk in so late. I then ask what time they would arrive if the ten o'clock appointment were a trip to the grocery store. In this case, my students would arrive "whenever" unless the store were about to close or there was a sale that ended shortly after ten o'clock. I finally ask them about a ten o'clock job interview or business meeting. Everyone then says they would arrive at least ten to fifteen minutes early because being late for such meetings could have disastrous career effects.

Imagine that you scheduled an international business meeting at ten o'clock, and some of the members didn't arrive until ten thirty. This is a common practice in many Latin American countries. As mentioned before, most business meetings in the United States "get to the point" immediately, but that is not the case in all areas of the world. In some countries, no actual business decisions, by United States standards, are made until a second or third meeting has been completed. In many areas of the world, time is a very fluid process, and not nearly as calculated and scheduled as it is in the United States (Morrison & Conaway, 2006). As a student of intercultural communication, understanding the possibilities of differences in these areas can make you an invaluable asset to any organization.

Organizational members are also influenced by cultural acceptance of how to *use* time. As we have discussed, the United States views time as a commodity, something that is either spent productively or wasted. Not surprisingly, a report by the Hudson recruitment firm (2007) found that half of workers in the United States don't use their vacation time. Of those who do,

35 percent of managers and 14 percent of nonmanagers still check in frequently with the office (sometimes daily) during their time off. This is not simply a U.S. trend. According to a different study by Hudson (Easen, 2005), nearly 80 percent of British executives expected to contact their office once a week during vacation, while 25 percent of them expected to contact the office daily. The United States is the only developed nation that does not mandate paid vacation for its workers. On the other hand, European countries guarantee a minimum of 20 days a year, and France tops the list with 31 days of annual paid vacation for its workers. In fact, the Austrian government values downtime so much it gives Austrians a tax break on the salary they earn while on vacation (Ravn, 2007).

As you can see, the concept of time in business differs drastically in many areas of the world in terms of how we use it, how we value it, how we pay for it, and whether or not we are paid for it. In the United States where time is a commodity, vacations are often seen as a "waste of time" because relaxation interferes with work. In other countries, this time is seen as a necessity for people to rest and relax so that they can be more productive at work.

Space

How seating is arranged in business meetings is an important aspect of intercultural communication within organizations. Where and how people sit and stand can be very different from culture to culture. In a low power distance country like the United States, it is customary for the person in charge to sit at the head of the table, but it is not essential. In fact, in many organizations, heads of companies may sit in the middle of the table to try to dissipate the notion of being "in charge" and encourage more open communication. However, in countries with a high power distance, like China, where there is a more distinct hierarchy, seniority tends to dictate where someone sits. In fact, not only is there a specific seat for the most senior person, but the rest of the seating is often precisely arranged by seniority and must be carefully adhered to. Certainly, sitting in the wrong seat can cause embarrassment, and maybe even impact future business dealings, but space can play an even more important role in how well a business does in another country. A study by Yan (2005) found that space is a key factor in determining the success of U.S.-based businesses overseas. In China, U.S.-style fast-food chains have done very well and become very popular with the local people, and one of the reasons for this is attributed to their space and layout. In the KFC and McDonald's in Beijing, China, both server and customer stand while the order is being placed, and customers are given quick tours of the clean, open kitchen so they can familiarize themselves with the food and the cooking process. The sense of equality between the server and the customer, as well as the openness of the space, makes the fast-food restaurants seem inviting and friendly, and is an important contributor to their success.

As you can see, space plays a vital role in how business is conducted, and also how well a business can do. By paying attention to cultural notions of space in organizations, students of intercultural communication have an edge in beginning to understand how business works both at home and across the globe.

REFERENCES

Anna, C. (2006, July 21). Schools juggle holidays for different faiths. *USA Today*.

Easen, N. (2005, August 5). Tied to the office on vacation. *CNN.com, World Business*. Retrieved from http://edition.cnn.com/2005/BUSINESS/08/05/tied.to.office/index.html

Morrison, T., & Conaway, W. A. (2006). *Kiss, bow, or shake hands* (2nd ed.). Avon, MA: Adams Media.

Ravn, K. (2007, July 16). In the U.S., all work and not much paid play. *Los Angeles Times*. Retrieved from http://articles.latimes.com/2007/jul/16/health/he-vacationsidde16

Smagorinski, P. (2001). If meaning is constructed, what is it made from? Toward a cultural theory of reading. *Review of Educational Research, 71*(1), 133–169.

U.S. Census Bureau (2000). *QT-P3: Race and Hispanic or Latino: 2000*. Retrieved from American FactFinder, http://factfinder.census.gov/servlet/ QTTable?_bm =y&-geo_id=01000US&-qr_name=DEC_2000_SF1_U_QTP3&-ds _name=DEC _2000_SF1_U&-redoLog=false

U.S. Census Bureau. (2003, February). *Married-couple and unmarried-partner households: 2000*. Retrieved from www.census.gov/prod/ 2003pubs/censr-5.pdf

U.S. Department of Justice. (1994). *ADA standards for accessible design*. Retrieved from http://www.ada.gov/stdspdf.htm

U.S. Department of Labor: Women's Bureau. (2005, November). *Employment status of women and men in 2005*. Retrieved from http://www.dol.gov/wb/factsheets/Qf-ESWM05.htm

Yan, Y. (2005). Of hamburger and social space: Consuming McDonald's in Beijing. In J. L. Watson & M. L. Caldwell (Eds.), *The cultural politics of food and eating: A reader* (pp. 80–103). Malden, MA: Blackwell Publishing.

Intercultural Communication 6
and Popular Culture

Where did you first learn about your own cultural traditions? How did you discover what other cultures are like? Most people don't learn about culture formally, especially when it comes to their own culture. We gain an understanding of it from the interactions and relationships with our parents, friends, and teachers. Despite these influences, the biggest "teacher" of culture is popular culture, which continuously surrounds us both in the forefront and in the background of our lives. Popular culture may be obvious to us in things like movies, books, and magazines, but we often don't notice the popular culture that is in the background—on billboards, at the grocery store, or even in our textbooks! That said, what is popular culture?

DEFINING POPULAR CULTURE

Defining popular culture is almost a study in itself, as there are many definitions and many arguments about what constitutes popular culture. In this text I define **popular culture** as "the range of media products, art forms and artifacts disseminated broadly in American society" (Laforse & Drake, 1981, p. viii). In other words, popular culture is a commodity (Fiske, 1989) intended to reach the widest range of people. A **commodity** is something that is bought and sold on an open market, usually with a price that is consistent with its demand. For example, we buy movies on DVD, we pay to rent movies, or we buy tickets to watch movies; thus movies are a commodity. However, even when a popular culture item itself isn't bought or sold by the public, it is still a commodity and has some function in the for-profit economy. Advertisements are a good example of this: you don't pay to watch or see advertisements (though others pay for you to see them), but they are still a commodity because they are presented to the public, and either consumed or rejected. Advertisements also encourage the consumption of popular culture commodities we do buy and sell, like movies, toys, and books.

Popular culture is so much a part of our everyday lives that we often don't pay attention to it. Take a moment to reflect on your day. Did you wake up to a clock radio? Turn on the TV? Are there any advertisements, posters, or billboards around you? Is your cell phone ringtone programmed with a popular song? If you answered "yes" to any of these, you have already experienced popular culture today, and it is unlikely that you even realized it.

POPULAR CULTURE AND OTHER FORMS OF CULTURE

Since popular culture encompasses so much of what is around us, it helps to understand the difference between popular culture and some other forms of culture. In this section we look at the differences between popular culture and folk culture, what constitutes high culture and low culture, and how both can be a part of popular culture.

Folk Culture

Folk culture is distinct from popular culture in that **folk culture** is made by the people for the people, and is not about the dissemination of ideas or products for profit. Many musicians make music simply for their own enjoyment, or to share within their own communities. Student filmmakers may make movies just for fun, or perhaps for a film festival on campus. These are examples of creating something without any notion of making a profit from it.

That's not to say that profit can't come into play. YouTube and other video-sharing sites are good examples; they are a fascinating mix of folk culture and popular culture. Certainly there are for-profit aspects to YouTube, and there are some scholars who argue that YouTube itself, and by extension, everything on it, is popular culture because it is commercial and widespread. While YouTube is a commercial site, it can give us some great examples of folk culture (Earl & Schussman, 2008), like the home videos that are posted exclusively for sharing with family members, even if they aren't marked for private viewing. In some cases, videos that began as personal videos posted on YouTube have inspired corporation-sponsored spin-offs of the original. For example, in 2003 a man named Matt Harding decided he would quit his job and travel around the world, and on this trip, a friend of his decided to video-tape Matt doing his signature dance in different places. The video was put on YouTube and got sent around from person to person over the Internet, eventually reaching the attention of the people at Stride gum. They loved his original video, and funded a trip in 2006 for Matt to travel and film himself dancing in even more countries, which led to even more YouTube fame, and a third video, also sponsored by Stride gum, in 2008.

Folk culture sometimes uses aspects of popular culture in ways they were not intended to be used. For instance, if you do a YouTube search for "I Hate Barney" you will probably find all sorts of portrayals of Barney that were never intended by PBS. Another example is the "Potter Puppet Pals" videos circulating on YouTube; while the characters of Harry Potter were created by J. K. Rowling for profit, a fan of the series created the videos featuring hand-made puppets of these characters for fun. When "for-profit" products are used by people to create their own nonprofit meanings and understandings, the new interpretations are considered folk culture. Though YouTube itself is based on profit, the majority of the videos that are posted are not.

High Culture and Low Culture

You may have also heard the terms "high culture" and "low culture" used as descriptors of certain activities. What constitutes "high culture" and "low culture" is based on class, taste, and trends (Gans, 1999). While it is a term used less frequently these days, **high culture** describes activities that are popular with, and highly valued by, the upper to upper-middle classes. Activities like the opera, the ballet, art museums, and public lectures are high culture activities because the upper to upper-middle classes can afford to spend the money required to attend those activities. Consequently, these activities have become tagged with the "elite" label, and participating in them has become almost required for those in the higher social classes. Gans (1999) posits these activities in opposition to those such as bowling, poker, and reading serial romance novels, which are categorized as **low culture** because they do not require much money to participate in and are therefore available and accessible to most people, especially those in the lower and middle classes.

How do high and low cultures relate to popular culture? In some cases, the terms "low culture" and "popular culture" are used interchangeably. However, in the study of intercultural communication, "popular culture" is anything that can be bought or sold that is disseminated to the masses, regardless of class or taste; therefore, something that is considered "high culture" can be as much a part of popular culture as something that is "low culture." For example, the *Mona Lisa* is classified as being part of "high culture" because it is fine art, but as the subject's infamous smile has been featured in advertisements and other consumer products, it can be seen as part of popular culture as well. NASCAR is an example of low culture that is also part of popular culture; certainly NASCAR-related and -endorsed products have been disseminated to the masses in a for-profit manner, but auto racing is also typically associated with the middle to lower economic classes. Both high culture and low culture, though different by definition, can be considered popular culture.

POPULAR CULTURE AND INTERCULTURAL COMMUNICATION

Now that we've discussed what does and does not constitute popular culture, we turn to a discussion of how it relates to intercultural communication and why intercultural scholars study it. Studying popular culture provides one way of looking at, and understanding, the symbols and meanings that make up culture. There are many ways to examine popular culture and many excellent books that explain theories of popular culture and how to use them to analyze popular culture objects and trends. However, for our purposes, we focus on examining popular culture to show us how, and what, we think about our own culture and others' cultures. What is communicated about different cultural groups in popular culture shapes how we view them. If stereotypical examples of "others" are all we see and are exposed to, we begin to think of them in a stereotypical fashion. For example, early portrayals of Asians in American film and television were very stereotypical. Asian women were portrayed as either extremely docile and subservient, or as seductive and evil— the "dragon lady" stereotype. Two common stereotypes of the Asian man were the "Charlie Chan" stereotype—an effeminate, harmless, polite man, and the "Fu Manchu" stereotype—the exotic and cruel face of the "yellow peril." People who were exposed only to these stereotypical portrayals may have believed that all Asians and Asian Americans fell strictly into those categories. Understand that even though not everyone in a particular group agrees with or condones how specific cultures, or aspects of cultures, are portrayed by popular culture, *meaning* is still created by popular culture, and it is important to understand what that meaning is.

There are many instances of intercultural communication to be found in popular culture, and while the examples I discuss are all U.S.-centric because of my background and familiarity with the United States, it's important to understand that the impact of popular culture is seen worldwide. Of course, some of these examples are more noticeable than others; we take a look at the difference between overt and covert intercultural communication next.

Overt Intercultural Communication

Intercultural communication is **overt** when the portrayals of cultures in popular culture, and the meaning of those portrayals, are obvious to the consumer. For example, if you look at commercials for cleaning products, they nearly always show females using the products, which reinforces the stereotype that women are supposed to be the ones taking care of the home. Certainly, research shows that women do more housework than men (Mixon, 2008), but women are also *depicted* in the media as doing more housework than men (Glascock & Preston-Schreck, 2004; Scharrer, Kim, Ke-Ming, Zixu, 2006), and viewing this stereotype in the media reinforces it. Signorielli and Lears (1992) showed that children's TV viewing habits strongly influenced their perceptions of which chores should be done by men and which should be done by women.

Also, in the early 2000s, the sitcom *Friends* was widely criticized for having an exclusively white cast, in essence portraying only white people as successful and upwardly mobile. *Friends* eventually added a recurring black character in 2003, but diversity on television continues to be a problem, with people of color significantly underrepresented in primetime (Media Matters, 2008; Henderson & Baldasty, 2003). A lack of portrayals of successful people of color in our mainstream media is problematic because it reinforces negative stereotypes. It is important not to underestimate the power and influence that the overt intercultural communication in popular culture wields.

Covert Intercultural Communication

On the other hand, intercultural communication is **covert** when the message contained in the portrayals of cultures in popular culture is hidden and less easy to recognize. You might have heard the word "covert" used in relation to top-secret CIA operations, but the difference between how "covert" is used in that sense and covert examples of intercultural communication is intention. Certainly, the CIA intends to keep its operations hidden and secret from others; much planning and money go into making sure these operations stay covert. However, it is rare that a film producer or toy maker thinks, "Hey, let's make sure this particular culture is framed as good or bad in our product, but let's not be obvious about it!" When there are hidden meanings in popular culture commodities, it is largely unintentional. Culture is constantly produced and reproduced around us, so we become oblivious to the norms of that culture — good or bad. For example, I've noticed that when stories about Latinos are covered on National Public Radio, there is often Latin music playing in the background at some point during the piece. While the act of playing the music is intentional, the meaning this choice conveys may not be one that the radio station intended. However, this background music still creates a covert message that is communicated along with the actual news story. The use of Latin music can unconsciously reinforce the "foreignness" of Latinos, even though Latinos have had a presence in the United States for multiple generations.

Covert messages are more insidious than overt messages. When a stereotypical message is overt, it is easier to pinpoint and, therefore, also easier to dismiss or be critical of. With covert messages, we tend to simply absorb them, without critically thinking about what the message is *really* saying. Even though covert messages may be unintended by the message sender, it is still important to be critical of those messages when we *do* notice them, especially if they are discriminatory or stereotypical. Not pointing them out means that these covert messages will likely continue to be reproduced and allowed.

ANALYZING POPULAR CULTURE MEDIA

Popular culture is disseminated to us in a variety of ways, every day. In the following section, I take a look at a few of those media, including television, films, books, and toys, and discuss how they convey certain ideas of culture to us, both overtly and covertly.

TELEVISION

More and more Americans are getting their information about the rest of the world from television. The U.S. census reported that in 2001 over 98 percent of households in the United States had a television set (U.S. Census Bureau, 2004), and channels like the Travel Channel have been contributing to the increasing diversification of television programming. Though people themselves may not travel to other countries, they can become "armchair travelers" through their television sets. Television has a great influence on how we see and understand other people, often without our even being aware of it. For example, Dixon and Linz (2000) found that African Americans and Latinos were much more likely to be shown as lawbreakers on television shows than whites. Most people might respond to this by arguing that they know the difference between fiction and reality. However, a study by Ford (1997) showed that people who watched a comedy skit featuring a negative portrayal of African Americans were then more likely to assume an African American to be guilty in a crime scenario that was read to them.

What Do We See Overtly in Television?

Overt examples of intercultural communication in television are abundant. One of my favorites to discuss is how gender roles in U.S. society are portrayed on television — especially the role of "father." In the episode "Debra's Sick" from the sitcom *Everybody Loves Raymond,* when Raymond's wife, Debra, becomes sick, he tries to take care of work and the house, but instead, chaos ensues. Similarly, in the episode "Rock-a-Bye, Bivalve" from the cartoon *SpongeBob SquarePants,* Patrick and SpongeBob adopt a baby clam together, and decide that SpongeBob will be the mother and Patrick will be the father. Patrick is portrayed as the stereotypical "absent father," for example, not returning from the office until late at night and relaxing in the easy chair in front of the television when he does get home, not doing household chores, and leaving SpongeBob, the "mom," to watch after the baby and the house.

Commercials that are shown on television also contain this message. In a McDonald's commercial, kids from all over the world run to tell their siblings that dad is making dinner. With that proclamation, everyone runs home, knowing that if dad "made" dinner, that means he has brought home McDonald's. There is also the Tyson Chicken commercial where the dad confesses to making frozen waffles when his wife is gone and he is left in charge of dinner. All of these are examples of the overt message of the father as a bumbling, inept caretaker. These common portrayals in a large segment of U.S. popular culture reflect how our culture views the role of the father and his relationship with children, as well as reinforce the prevailing idea that the role of the father doesn't include being able to cook, clean, or change a diaper.

What Do We See Covertly in Television?

There are also plenty of examples of covert messages on television. Let's look at an example of one about gender. In the popular children's cartoon

Kim Possible, the lead character, Kim Possible, seems to be a great role model for girls—she is a cheerleader by day and a superhero by night. Though she is quick-witted and uses numerous gadgets to defeat her enemies, the show's story line often focuses on Kim's crushes. For example, in the episode "Exchange," an exchange student, Hirotaka, comes from Japan to Kim's school while Kim's friend and comic-relief sidekick Ron gets sent to a secret ninja school in Japan. Ron ends up defeating the enemies threatening to take over the school, while Kim ends up using her gadgetry to locate Hirotaka so she can ask him out on a date. In this example, the overt image of the strong, intelligent girl is undermined when Kim uses her brains simply to get a boy to notice her, while Ron is the one who does the physical fighting to defeat the enemies. This episode sends the message that girls, ultimately, are only focused on boys and crushes. This is considered a covert message because of the cartoon's intended and advertised message of "girl as superhero." On first glance, we may think that Kim Possible is a healthy role model for young girls who watch the show, but until we examine the covert message critically, we may not realize what else young girls are absorbing along with the overt message.

FILM

Film has become a large part of life in many parts of the world; in 2007, 1.42 billion tickets to the movies were sold (Barnes, 2008). Not only do movies reflect societies' views of cultures—their own and others—at the time they're made, they can shape how people see and talk about those cultures. Certainly, film has played a major role in showing and shaping a society's views on race. Over time, films in the United States have moved from having few characters of color to featuring some people of color in leading roles. In some ways this reflects changes in our society: the United States has become more accepting of people of color. Also, seeing people of color in diverse roles on the silver screen has allowed the United States, as a society, to accept people of color in more varied roles in real life. In fact, some have argued that the black men who played U.S. presidents in film, like James Earl Jones and Morgan Freeman, helped to pave the way for Barack Obama's presidency (NPR, 2008; Ogunniake, 2008)!

What Do We See Overtly in Film?

When we think of overt messages in film, one of the most noticeable is the racial portrayal of "good guys" and "bad guys." A large number of films in the United States portray people of color in the role of the villain, while white people are typically depicted as heroes. Examples of this are found in *Lethal Weapon 4* (1998), where Asians are primarily depicted as gang members who know martial arts, and in *Training Day* (2001), where African Americans are mainly portrayed as gang members, corrupt police officers, and drug dealers.

The lack of films featuring stories *about* people of color is also a significant overt message in film. There are many popular films that center around white people, like *Juno* (2007), *Harry Potter and the Goblet of Fire* (2007), and *There Will Be Blood* (2007). However, of Roger Ebert's picks for the top ten movies of 2007, there were only two films that told the story of people of color: *Kite Runner* (2007), which centered on a young boy of Middle Eastern descent, and *The Great Debaters* (2007), about an African American debate team. People of color are often secondary characters, and even if they are central characters, they rarely carry a film's plot on their own — they often have partners or sidekicks (Gates, 2004). If audiences repeatedly watch primarily negative depictions of a specific group, these stereotypes can become ingrained, and communication is affected (Berg, 2002).

What Do We See Covertly in Film?

Just as we saw in television, films can also contain covert messages that reflect and influence popular culture. For example, the Disney film *Aladdin* (1992) appears to be set in the Middle East, with a full cast of Middle Eastern characters (albeit in cartoon form). However, if you examine the way Aladdin and Jasmine are portrayed more critically, you may notice that they both have midwestern American accents, while Jafar, the villain, has a decidedly different, foreign-sounding accent (though not exactly Middle Eastern either!). Also, Aladdin and Jasmine both have stereotypical Caucasian features, such as small noses and light-colored skin — in fact, Aladdin was modeled after Tom Cruise! Jafar, on the other hand, has caricatured Middle Eastern features — his nose is much larger than the other characters, and his skin is also much darker (Giroux, 1997). Due to the fact that, at first glance, the characters seem like they are all part of the same race, and because the racial traits used to differentiate good from evil are more subtle, the stereotypes that exist in this film may often go unnoticed. However, like the examples of overt messages discussed above, *Aladdin* positions the "person of color" character as evil and the "Caucasian" characters as good, and reinforces the stereotypes about people of color that may already exist in people's minds.

BOOKS

When thinking about the place of books in popular culture, people may assume that only fiction counts as popular culture. However, all books are part of popular culture, regardless of whether they are romance novels or college textbooks, and they all have cultural significance. For example, the very fact that the Gutenberg Bible was the first mass-produced book speaks to the importance of religion and the desire to spread the knowledge of Christianity during the 1400s. What books do and don't show certainly reflects a society's views of culture. Because books are a key tool in education, it is even more important to look at books as *shaping* societal views.

What Do We See Overtly in Books?

Let's look at the overt messages that books can send by looking at the omissions in books. This might seem like an odd way of determining what books tell us about a society's understanding of their culture and others' cultures, but I believe that what is excluded is often more telling than what is included. For instance, there is a distinct absence of portrayals of children of color and of children with differing abilities in many picture books. Of the top-ten children's books of 2007 listed in *Time* magazine, only two featured people of color as main characters. The top-ten best-selling children's books as listed by *Publishers Weekly* for the week of September 15, 2007, listed only one book that featured a person of color as a main character. What are the ramifications of these omissions? Certainly, one of the consequences is that children who are of a race other than white may feel that, because they see no representation of themselves in American books, they are not valued in American society. Also, when there are very few depictions of people of color or other underrepresented groups, people can come away from the reading experience picturing people of color or other minority groups only in stereotypical roles (Rasinski & Padak, 1998). This is not to say that all of the books that include people of color or other minority groups cast them in stereotypical roles only, but when there is heavy *omission* of these groups from books, there are fewer, and less varied, examples out there to act as a counterpoint to the stereotypical examples that do exist.

What Do We See Covertly in Books?

Identifying the covert messages in children's books can show the contradictions between overt messages and what is *really* being conveyed. Let's look at *Whoever You Are* by Mem Fox (1997), a popular children's book, as an example. This book has drawings portraying children from all over the world, and its intent is to show that, while these children may be different from the reader, they are really "just like" the reader. However, there are covert messages conveyed by the illustrations in the book that contradict that aim. For example, one page of the book shows an Asian girl, an African boy, a Latina girl, and a Caucasian boy, and behind each of the children is a depiction of their homes. The Asian girl is pictured with houses that have roofs with dramatic curlicues at each corner, the African boy is pictured with houses with grass or straw roofs, and the Latina girl is pictured with houses featuring adobe-tiled roofs. However, the Caucasian boy is pictured with modern-looking skyscrapers and houses with triangle-shaped roofs and chimneys. Throughout the book, things that look modern and urban are paired almost exclusively with Caucasian children, whereas the children of color are typically shown with things that appear "exotic." While the text in the book does point out that "their skin may be different from yours, and their homes may be different from yours" (p. 4), they are illustrated in such a stereotypical way that it highlights and fetishizes difference, rather than conveying the message that although there are differences between people all over the world, we are all, essentially, equal. As readers, we may not be conscious of the fact that the two messages are contradictory, and so we absorb, and accept, both.

TOYS

In the United States alone, people spent more than 22 billion dollars on toys in 2007 (NPD Group, 2008), and they are a central part of the lives of most children. Many people have fond memories of the toys they grew up with, and toys often act as a reflection of the popular trends of specific time periods. My Little Pony was all the rage in the 1980s, Power Rangers action figures and Super Soaker water guns took over in the 1990s, and Pokémon trading cards and video games dominated in the early 2000s. What toys are created when, and how they're received by the public, certainly send a message about a society's cultural views.

What Do We See Overtly in Toys?

One of the more overt messages that toys send is in regard to gender and sexuality. This is certainly evident in the toys that are intended for, and marketed at, the different genders: boys are "supposed" to play with action figures, while girls are "supposed" to play with dolls. The toys themselves also conform to strict stereotypes of gender expression and gender roles. For example, dolls targeted at girls are almost always dressed in pink or purple, and, while G. I. Joe is incredibly popular, G. I. Jane was quickly discontinued. In terms of sexuality, the vast majority of commercially available dolls are coded to be heterosexual. Perhaps the most famous dolls of all, Ken and Barbie, were designed to conform to multiple cultural standards in the United States, like standards of dress, standards of work, and standards of gender (Caldas-Coulthard & van Leeuwen, 2002). But while Barbie's occupations have expanded past traditionally "female" ones since her inception, both Barbie and Ken still conform to strict standards of heteronormativity — Barbie has never had a girlfriend, and Ken has never had a boyfriend. However, there was a short period in 1993 when Mattel introduced "Earring Magic Ken," a doll who had an earring and a lilac colored vest, and the doll was widely embraced by the gay community. However, due to public outcry over the doll's supposed homosexuality, "Earring Magic Ken" was discontinued after a short time, despite being the best-selling Ken doll in Mattel history (Jones, 2002; "Barbie: A Life," 2002). There is only one openly gay doll on the market — the Billy doll — and he is not widely available commercially. The fact that there is no market in the mainstream toy industry for toys that deviate from the "norm" of heterosexuality sends the message to children that heterosexuality is the only acceptable, and socially condoned, form of sexual orientation.

What Do We See Covertly in Toys?

Toys also send covert messages that reflect our society and our views on specific cultures. As I've mentioned before, omissions reflect a lot about a society's views of culture, and while toy manufacturers do try to address some omissions, like creating African American and Hispanic versions of the Barbie doll, sometimes there are covert messages that contradict their overt message of inclusiveness. Let's look at the availability of differently abled dolls as an example of this. There are very few dolls or action figures available on the market that have differing abilities, and those that are available are not widely produced. In 1996, as a means of addressing this, Mattel introduced Barbie's friend, "Share a Smile Becky," who uses a wheelchair. However, Mattel soon ran into problems when it was discovered that Becky was unable to fit through the doors of the "Barbie Dream House" because they were too small to accommodate her wheelchair ("Barbie's Disabled Friend," 1997). This shows the contradiction between the overt message and the covert message: Mattel's intent was to show how sensitive they were to differing abilities, but the doll's limited access undercuts that message. This example certainly reflects our society's neglect of differently abled people's needs because there are many places in the United States that are either inaccessible or difficult to access by people who are differently abled. Toys are key to children's education about the society and culture they live in. Often, children will use dolls or action figures to act out or imitate real-life scenarios, so if a child cannot fit Becky through the doors of a house, they may just assume that it is "normal" for dolls and, by extension, for people in wheelchairs to not be able to fit through doors.

REFERENCES

Barbie: A life in plastic. (2002, December 19). *The Economist, 365*(8304).

Barbie's disabled friend can't fit. (1997). *Associated Press*. Retrieved from http://www.washington.edu/doit/Press/barbie.html

Barnes, B. (2008, January 2). A film year full of escapism, flat in attendance. *The New York Times*. Retrieved from http://www.nytimes.com

Berg, C. R. (2002). *Latino images in film: Stereotypes, subversion, and resistance.* Austin: University of Texas Press.

Caldas-Coulthard, C. R., van Leeuwen, T. (2002). Stunning, shimmering, iridescent: Toys as the representation of gendered social actors. In L. Litosseliti & J. Sunderland (Eds.), *Gender identity and discourse analysis* (pp. 91–110). Philadelphia: John Benjamins.

Dixon, T., & Linz, D. (2000). Overrepresentation and underrepresentation of African Americans and Latinos as lawbreakers on television news. *Journal of Communication, 50,* 131–154.

Earl, J., & Schussman, A. (2008). Contesting cultural control: Youth culture and online petitioning. In L. W. Bennett (Ed.), *Civic life online: Learning how digital media can engage youth* (pp. 71–95). Cambridge, MA: MIT Press.

Fiske, J. (1989). *Understanding popular culture.* New York: Routledge.

Ford, T. E. (1997). Effects of stereotypical television portrayals of African-Americans on person perception. *Personality and Social Psychology Quarterly, 60,* 266–275.

Gans, Herbert J. (1999). *Popular culture and high culture: An analysis and evaluation of taste.* New York: Basic Books

Gates, P. (2004). Always a partner in crime: Black masculinity in the Hollywood detective film. *Journal of Popular Film and Television, 32*(1), 20–29.

Giroux, H. (1997). Are Disney movies good for your kids? In S. R. Steinberg & J. L. Kincheloe (Eds.), *Kinderculture: The corporate construction of childhood.* Boulder, CO: Westview Press.

Glascock, J., & Preston-Schreck, C. (2004). Gender and racial stereotypes in daily newspaper comics: A time-honored tradition? *Sex Roles, 51,* 423–431.

Henderson, J. J., & Baldasty, G. J. (2003). Race, advertising, and prime-time television. *Howard Journal of Communications, 14*(2), 97–112.

Jones, A. (2002). *The feminism and visual culture reader.* New York: Routledge

Laforse, M. W., & Drake, J. A. (1981). *Popular culture and American life: Selected topics in the study of twentieth century American popular culture.* Chicago: Burnham.

Media Matters for America. (2008, July). Gender and ethnic diversity in prime-time cable news. Retrieved from http://mediamatters.org/reports/diversity_report/

Mixon, B. (2008, April 28). Chore wars: Men, women and housework. *National Science Foundation: Discoveries.* Retrieved from http://www.nsf.gov/discoveries/disc_summ.jsp?cntn_id=111458

NPD Group. (2008, June 3). *More households purchased toys in the U.S. last year than in 2006* [Press release]. Retrieved from http://www.npd.com/press/releases/press_080603a.html

NPR. (2008, January 31). Has Hollywood helped pave the way for Obama? *All things considered.* Retrieved from http://www.npr.org/templates/story/story.php?storyId =18580711

Ogunnaike, L. (2008, June 5). Black presidents nothing new to Hollywood. *CNN.com.* Retrieved from http://www.cnn.com

Rasinski, T. V., & Padak, N. D. (1998). Multicultural learning through children's literature. In M. F. Opitz (Ed.), *Literacy instruction for culturally and linguistically diverse students: A collection of articles and commentaries.* Newark, DE: International Reading Association.

Scharrer, E. D., Kim, D., Ke-Ming, L., & Zixu, L. (2006). Working hard or hardly working? Gender, humor, and the performance of domestic chores in television commercials. *Mass Communication & Society, 9*(2), 215–238.

Signorielli, N., & Lears, M. (1992). Children, television, and conceptions about chores: Attitudes and behaviors. *Sex Roles, 27*(3–4), 157–170.

U.S. Census Bureau. (2004, March 11). *50th anniversary of 'Wonderful World of Color' TV* (Release No. CB04-FFSE.04). Retrieved from http://www.census.gov/Press-Release/www/releases/archives/facts_for_features_special_editions/001702.html

Wrapping It Up: 7
Why Intercultural
Communication Matters

When I decided to take on the project of writing this book I did it for a reason. I wanted to be able to talk to students about intercultural communication—how important I think it is and how fascinating it can be. Certainly governments engage in intercultural communication, and it is a vital aspect of their work that has the potential to affect the world, for good or for bad, yet it is also something that is at work in our own lives. We live our lives in a cultural manner, even when we don't realize it. Intercultural communication is continually in flux; our language evolves to include new words and meanings ("cool," "phat"), and world events may change how we think of ourselves and others (9/11, for example). As a result, we are forced to constantly look at something new and think about it in a critical manner, which can often be interesting and sometimes even fun! Our attitudes toward intercultural communication, that is, what we pay attention to and what we choose to address, are even more significant. Such attitudes can affect not just individuals, but society at large, as well as the next generation.

In order to show students how important it is to be engaged with intercultural communication, I like to tell them the story of my car. I have a pretty beat-up car. It's ten years old, the driver's window has duct tape on it, and there are melted crayon markings on the backseat. One day I was driving to work, and I heard a very strange noise coming from the engine. When I got to class I asked my students what I should do about it. They nearly unanimously decided I should take my car to the mechanic to get looked at. Those who didn't agree said I should just give up and junk it. I stood there, thoughtfully, and told them I decided against their advice. Instead, I was going to simply turn up the car radio until I couldn't hear the noise anymore. My response left the students dumbfounded. I could actually see a few of them in the first row rolling their eyes. Others called back at me, "You're crazy!"; "You're going to get yourself in trouble!" I looked at them with wide-eyed ignorance and asked them why they were so upset. They explained to me that if I ignored the problem it would just get worse, and eventually I wouldn't be able to fix it.

At this point I stopped to agree with their argument. I then pointed out that we could make the same case regarding intercultural communication. Though internationally we have come very far in the realm of intercultural communication, there is still a long way to go. There are still hate crimes committed against people because of how they look, how they talk, who they date, where they come from, and what God (if any) they worship. Even without hate crimes, people are treated differently depending on their characteristics. If we turn up the radio and ignore these problems, they are going to get worse. It may seem unimaginable that we could erase the strides we have made in intercultural communication, but they can be erased. Unless we remain vigilant. Unless we refuse to turn up the radio.

This may seem like an easy thing to accomplish, but it's not. When we are not forced into intercultural situations every day, it is very easy to ignore them. It is easy to laugh at a movie without being critical of what you see culturally. It's easy to laugh at an off-color joke when everyone else around you laughs, and when it isn't about you. If you are white in the United States, in many parts of the country it's easy to ignore, or not even notice, the fact that everyone around you looks like you. In most places in the United States, if you are white, most of the students in your class may look like you. Your teachers may look like you. The mail carrier may look like you. If you are in the United States and Christian, most of the people around you may worship like you do. If you are heterosexual, most people date and marry like you do. It is easy to forget about people who are different from you if they are not around you, and if their difference isn't easily visible.

As a student of intercultural communication, not turning up the radio means noticing these things. It means noticing them, talking about them, and addressing them. I don't like taking my car into the shop. I know every time I do, it's an inconvenience. I know every time I do, it's going to cost money — probably a lot of money. But I do it anyway because I know in the long run it's going to cost less than the alternative. The same thing applies to addressing intercultural communication issues. It's an inconvenience. It means looking at things in a way you haven't before, which can be a pain. I have students who complain to me after class that they can't just sit back and watch a TV show anymore. They are continually analyzing it. Addressing intercultural communication is expensive too. It can cause you embarrassment. It can cost you friends. But in the long run, the costs can be greater—personally, nationally, globally.

So what should we do? What are some ways we can address issues of intercultural communication in our everyday lives? Here are five things to remember regarding intercultural communication.

TOP-FIVE THINGS TO REMEMBER

Remembering these five things can help students of intercultural communication battle against the desire to turn up the radio. If we remember these things, we can help make our lives, and the lives of others around us, just a little bit better.

1. INTERCULTURAL COMMUNICATION IS *EVERYWHERE*.

There is very little we do that doesn't communicate something. There is also very little we do that isn't associated with culture. How we walk, how we talk, how we smile, what we like, what we don't, how we dress, how we speak—all of these are aspects of intercultural communication.

Communicate—It's Great!

When we remember how much communication surrounds us, we are bound to become better communicators. We become aware of how we and others communicate, and this helps us understand the differences among us. Political correctness is the hit word of the day with its message of "Be nice to people, say the right thing." While this idea is good, there is a big problem with how political correctness is often approached. Yes, we should all be nice to people. Yes, we should be polite, courteous, and respectful. However, the important thing to remember is to *communicate*. All too often, people avoid intercultural communication completely because they aren't sure what the "correct" thing is to say. So, they say *nothing*. In order to understand other people, we *must* communicate. If we don't talk to people because we aren't sure what to say, there is no hope of solving any intercultural differences— perceived or real—that exist. So communicate. Always communicate.

2. NORMAL ISN'T NORMAL AT ALL.

One of the most important themes that runs through this book is that there is no such thing as "normal" when it comes to intercultural communication. The root word for normal is "norm," which implies a constant average, but normal is only defined by what we're used to. I remember watching the 2008 Olympics in Beijing on television and seeing an interview with some visiting people from the United States who complained about the snack foods avail- able at the Olympic venues. The snack they liked best was popcorn! The fried starfish and sticky rice with sweet filling offered as snacks by some of the Chi- nese street vendors were not considered by many people from the United States to be snacks (or even foods!) since they weren't "normal" to them.

Remember, There Is No Such Thing as "Normal."

Realizing that there is no such thing as "normal" will help you see the communication of others in a whole new light. How so? This realization means we understand that what others do may be different, but that different does not equate to "bad" or "weird"; it's just different. This can only help intercultural communication because it makes us more tolerant of others. Realizing that there is no such thing as "normal" also means that the common excuse, "but that's just the way it's always been!" for why we do, or say, the things we do is no longer a valid one. We are able to critically look at our own communications once we remove ourselves from the "normalcy" trap.

3. BORDERS ARE EVERYWHERE — EVEN AT THE CONVENIENCE STORE.

We don't just encounter borders when we cross into cities or countries. We encounter borders every day. They are in our neighborhood as we go down different streets, they are around the corner at the place of worship, and they are even down the road at the shopping mall. When you walk down the street and see things written in a different language, that may be a cultural border. When you encounter a family celebrating a birthday or holiday very differently from the way you do, that is a border. Borders, those that are obvious and those that are more subtle, surround us.

Dare to Cross Some Borders.

Are you a part of a student organization on campus? Which one? Are you part of the Gay Lesbian Bisexual Transgendered group? How about the Latino Student Organization? What about Hillel? If you read any of these and answered: "No, I don't join those groups because I'm not (gay, Latino, Jewish)," it's time you thought about crossing some borders. These groups do not exist solely for membership within their own cultural groups. Just like your campus environmental group, these groups welcome people from all cultures. These groups welcome people from all walks of life because they understand that when people are willing to learn about cultures that are different from their own, it has a positive effect on everyone. Joining a student organization is an ideal way to cross some borders and develop a greater understanding of intercultural communication. If you are uncomfortable crossing these borders, try some smaller ones first. Find places that you don't usually go into (an ethnic food market, for example), and explore! Crossing borders often seems like a scary prospect because we don't know what to expect, but if we can put aside the fear of the unknown and listen to other cultures, we can help bridge cultural differences and improve intercultural communication.

4. BARBIE IS MORE THAN JUST A PRETTY FACE.

Popular culture is probably one of the most important aspects of intercultural communication, but in some ways it is also one of the most invisible. We are so used to going to see a movie, listening to music, or buying toys for kids in the family that we often think nothing of what we're consuming. However, there are many cultural messages embedded in these aspects of popular culture. For example, Barbie isn't just a pretty doll for girls, she is a cultural icon that tells girls how they should look, what they should be when they grow up (Barbie has had over forty jobs in her life), and whom they should date. While it may seem like we're reading "too much" into toys, these messages make popular culture incredibly powerful in intercultural communication.

Consume Diverse Items.

Do you have a little cousin, a niece or nephew, or another child in your life whom you might buy gifts for? If so, think about buying items that represent and feature a diverse range of cultures. There are a number of multicultural toys, movies, and books on the market that feature different religions, different types of relationships, differences in ethnicity, and differences in ability. One day, one of my daughters—who loves ballet—came out crying from her second day of dance class because she was afraid of a little girl in the class who had Downs Syndrome. She had never seen anyone with Downs Syndrome and had no idea what to expect. We looked for children's books that showed people with Downs Syndrome and talked to her about the little girl in her dance class. Once she had some understanding of how this little girl was and wasn't different from her, she was fine and enjoyed dancing in class with her classmate. What this story shows is that children do learn about the world around them through play, and that exposing children to concepts of intercultural communication through popular culture will encourage their own communications with people of other cultural backgrounds. You may have to keep an eye out for these items—they aren't always as easy to find, but think about how that could change if we bought more of them! You can use your purchasing power to make sure there is more demand for, and hence, supply of, multicultural products for sale.

5. THINGS AREN'T ALWAYS WHAT THEY SEEM TO BE.

People make assumptions. It helps us get along in the world—like assuming the weather forecast will be (mostly) right, so we can dress properly for our day. But we also have to be careful when we make assumptions. What we assume to be true is not always the case. Remember the local bar in my college town that had a "Latino Night"? Well, I was talking to this Latino guy there once, and trying to make a good impression. We were discussing a Latino-centered TV show that had a lot of embedded cultural meaning in it and I said, "Well, you're Mexican, so you'll understand that one part where . . . ." He stopped me and said, firmly but kindly, "I am not Mexican. I am Puerto Rican and Nicaraguan. You can't assume just because someone has brown skin that they are Mexican." Open mouth, insert foot. It was a big cultural boo-boo to be sure, but in the end, I married him!

Don't Be Afraid to Make Mistakes.

It's okay to make mistakes—even big ones—in fact, I guarantee you *will* make them! It certainly won't be the end of the world or even the end of a romantic relationship or friendship. Rather, if you approach each situation with respect and truly try to learn from everyone, people will generally be gracious and understanding. By keeping your eyes, ears, and mind open, you can learn from those mistakes—and the mistakes of others—so you don't repeat them. On the other hand, if you are afraid to make mistakes, you are much more likely to fall into the trap of not communicating—which is the most dangerous trap. When you don't communicate, you turn up the radio. When you turn up the radio, you ignore problems that are brewing, which can make things worse.

A FINAL WORD

Intercultural communication is important to me for a number of reasons, but in particular it means something to me because of my kids' future. As a mother of biracial children, I want my kids to grow up in a world that is free of prejudice. I know this is an unreasonable demand, because they have already been affected by many of these issues and because the world can never really be completely free of prejudice, but I want to make facing these issues easier for them. There are two ways I can do that. The first is to talk to them about these issues, to help them understand how outside forces might try to impinge upon their identities. The second is to talk to others about intercultural communication, to talk to people about differences among others in religion, ability, sexuality, and race, and to explore with others what kinds of meaning those issues have in our everyday lives.

So what does this mean to you? You certainly don't know my kids. But you may have nieces or nephews, brothers or sisters, or friends who have young children around them. You may have children, or you may wish to have children some day. Talking to them and others in your life about intercultural communication helps to make this world a better place. When we remember how our actions affect others—from how we speak to what products we consume, it makes a difference. When we remember that what is normal and comfortable for us may not be for others, and that other ways are just as "right" as our way, that makes a difference. Simply having a conversation about issues in intercultural communication makes a difference, and not just in the lives of the next generation. It doesn't matter what age you are, you can always learn something new about intercultural communication. It isn't easy, and at times it may feel like all you do is encounter roadblocks and pitfalls. It may feel easier to give up, and not challenge or fight any of the prejudices or discriminatory practices that exist, but I'll be the first one to tell you to keep fighting. Go talk about it. Communicate with others, and be an example of what intercultural communication can be in the world.

GLOSSARY

accent How we pronounce different vowel and consonant sounds in particular combinations.

acceptance The second stage in majority identity development where majority group members have some awareness of the privileges they have over those in minority groups.

ascribed identities Identities that others attribute to us.

assimilation This occurs when the immigrant completely adopts the host culture as his or her own.

avowal identities Identities that we choose to associate with and portray.

bounded intercultural relationship A relationship with cultural differences defined by the individuals involved although these differences may not be recognized by others.

chronemics The study of how we use time.

commodity Something that is bought and sold on an open market, usually with a price that is consistent with its demand.

communication The symbolic exchange of meaningful verbal and nonverbal messages.

conformity The second stage in minority identity development, where adoption and acceptance of the beliefs and values of the dominant culture occur.

covert When, during intercultural communication, the message contained in the portrayals of cultures in popular culture is hidden and less easy to recognize.

cultural borders Places where we encounter cultural differences in our everyday lives, not necessarily designated by geography.

culture Socially constructed meanings and symbols that are passed down from generation to generation.

culture shock The feelings of anxiety and disorientation some experience upon arriving in a new cultural environment due to the lack of familiar cues.

discrimination This occurs when negative beliefs or feelings about a group of people are acted on.

dominant intercultural relationships Relationships with cultural differences that are readily recognized by society.

ethnic identity An aspect of cultural identity that involves someone's national and/or cultural heritage.

fad An idea or item that is enthusiastically followed or coveted by a group of people, but only for a short amount of time.

folk culture Products or ideas that are made by the people for the people, and are not for profit.

gender The socially constructed idea of what is masculine and feminine.

generational Something that is passed down in society from generation to generation.

geographic borders Borders that separate one area of land from another, and are determined by people.

greeting scripts Understandings for how to meet others in a polite manner.

haptics The study of touch.

harassment Communication that intends to hurt or offend an individual, creating a hostile environment.

high culture Activities that require a good amount of money to participate in, thus are popular with, and highly valued by, the upper to upper-middle classes.

high power distance Describes a society in which people expect hierarchy and status to matter.

high touch cultures Cultures that use touch frequently in interpersonal interactions.

human trafficking The coerced recruitment, transportation, harboring, or receipt of people for the purpose of exploitation, slavery, or forced labor.

identity How we view ourselves, as well as how others view us. It is everchanging and complex.

indirect style of communication A style of communication where speakers purposefully do not directly state their main point out of respect to the person they are speaking with.

institutional When something is built into our institutions: into our schools, into our organizations, into our government, and into the whole of our society.

integration (Chapter 3) The fourth and final stage in minority and majority identity development where members of the minority group come to an understanding that there are positives and negatives in both the majority and minority cultures, and members of the majority group understand the privilege that is held by their group and work toward a more equal society.

integration (Chapter 4) This is a blend of assimilation and separation.

intercultural communication Communication with or about people of different cultural groups.

intercultural relationship This occurs when two people of different cultural backgrounds come together in a mutual connection.

internalized When cultural performances or symbols become so instinctive that we don't see them and we don't think about them—they simply exist within us.

intimate space A proxemic zone, from zero to eighteen inches.

involuntary immigrants Those who are forced by either people or circumstances to leave their home countries.

language Words or symbols that are governed by a grammatical system.

looking glass theory Charles Cooley's theory that how we see ourselves is shaped by how we think others see us.

low culture Activities that do not require much money to participate in, and therefore are available and accessible to most people, especially those in the lower and middle classes.

low power distance Describes a society in which people expect to be viewed largely as equals.

low touch cultures Cultures that avoid touch in most interpersonal interactions.

marginalization This occurs when an immigrant's desire for integration is rejected by the host culture.

middle touch cultures Cultures that use touch less frequently than high touch cultures, but more frequently than low touch cultures.

monochronic A word describing the view that time is linear and constantly moving forward and the past is generally thought of as having little impact on everyday goings-on.

nonverbal communication Communication that takes place without the use of language.

organizations Groups with a formal governance and structure including (but not limited to) businesses, governments, educational institutions, religious institutions, and nonprofits.

overt When, during intercultural communication, the portrayals in popular culture, and the meaning of those portrayals, are obvious to the consumer.

perception How we interpret and understand a message.

personal space A proxemic zone, from eighteen inches to four feet.

pidgin language A simplified and unifying language that is created by melding two different languages.

political correctness Speaking or acting in an inoffensive manner, especially with regard to race, religion, sexual orientation, and so on.

polychronic A word describing the view that time is more flexible and cyclical, and that past events have an impact on the present and the future.

popular culture Ideas, products, and art forms that are in vogue and widely disseminated to society through a variety of channels.

prejudices Typically negative beliefs or attitudes about a group of people, based on little or no evidence.

proxemics The study of the invisible bubble of space around us, or what is commonly known as our "personal space."

proxemic zones Zones of personal space.

public space A proxemic zone, over twelve feet.

racial identity An aspect of cultural identity that involves the race with which an individual identifies and/or the race with which others identify that person.

racism An act of discrimination aimed at a particular racial group.

redefinition The fourth stage in majority identity development where majority group members not only recognize the inequalities between majority and minority groups, but actively fight against their own privilege.

reentry shock The temporal, psychological difficulties involved are similar to those of culture shock, but this occurs when a traveler returns to his or her home culture after having lived in the host culture for a significant time.

resistance The third stage in majority identity development, where members of the majority group blame themselves for the discrepancies between the majority and the minority groups.

resistance and separatism The third stage in minority identity development, where minority group members become disillusioned with, and turn their backs on, the majority culture.

separation This occurs when the immigrant completely rejects (as much as possible) the host culture and any overtures to join it.

sex Our chromosomal makeup and biologically assigned reproductive organs.

sexism An act of discrimination toward a particular sex or gender.

social construction Something that is created by a society.

social space A proxemic zone, from four feet to twelve feet.

stereotypes Specific generalizations about a group of people that can be positive or negative.

symbol Something that represents, or is associated with, something else.

u-curve model A model that describes how travelers go through various stages of cultural adjustment, starting off on a high note, then going down into culture shock and periods of despair, and finally going back up into cultural adjustment and/or adaptation.

unexamined identity The first stage in both minority and majority identity development, where an individual doesn't recognize or isn't interested in issues of identity.

verbal communication Communication that uses language.

voluntary immigrants Those who migrate of their own free will.

w-curve model An alternative model for the cultural adjustment process that begins in the same way as the u-curve model, but then repeats itself to show a similar experience upon reentry to the home culture.

INDEX